BONSAI

Grow Your Own Little Japanese Zen Garden

A Beginner's Guide On How To Cultivate And Care For Your Bonsai Trees

by
Akira Kobayashi - 小林明

Image by Ilona Ilyés from Pixabay
Pixabay License
Free for commercial use
No attribution required

- ASIN : B08HTBB6NW paperback
- ASIN: B08LSKB1DG kindle
- Language : English
- Paperback : 212 pages
- ISBN-13 : 979-8685857057

Published by DARING LTD

Grab Spanish Edition U.S. Market

Grab Spanish Edition U.K. Market

Grab Spanish Edition ES Market

Grab Spanish Edition MX Market

SOMMARIO

Introduction 9

Chapter 1 - The principles of bonsai art 13

Chapter 2 - How to grow bonsai 20
    Recovered in nature or Yamadori 21
    Cultivation from seed or Misho 27
    Multiplication by cuttings or Sashiki 32
    Multiplication by layering or Toriki 39
    Propagation by grafting or Tsugiki 43
    Nursery Bonsai 48
    How to attach bonsai to your container 50

Chapter 3 - Bonsai and its styles 58
    Single styles 60
    Group styles 71
    Both single and group bonsai styles 79
    Ishitsuki or rocky style 81
    Saikei and Bonkei 85

Chapter 4 - Bonsai care 88
    Pruning 90
        Structural Pruning 92
        Maintenance Pruning 96
        Cutting leaves and buds 97
    Application of the metal wire 100
        Types of Wires 101
        How to Wire Your Bonsai 101
    Watering and Fertilizing 105
        Successful Watering 105
        Successful Fertilizing 109

Chapter 5 - Plant diseases 112
    Animal and plant pests 114
    Problems due to the environment 129
    Diseases due to excess or lack of nutrients 134
    Injuries and wounds 136
Chapter 6 - Containers and tools 137
Arrangement of bonsai in the container 139
Bonsai tools 141
Chapter 7 - Tips and information 144
Chapter 8 – 54-Plants datasheets 147
    ARALIA MING (Polyscias fructicosa) 148
    AZALEA (Azalea indica) 149
    BAMBOO (Bambusa humilis) 150
    BEECH (Fagus sylvatica) 151
    BIRCH (Betula nigra) 152
    BOX-TREE (Buxus harlandii) 153
    BUGANVILLEA (Bougainvillea glabra) 154
    CAMELLIA JAPONICA (Camelia japonica) 155
    CHERRY OF THE ANTILLES (Malpighia coccigera) 156
    CHINESE ELM (Ulmus parvifolia) 157
    CHRISTMAS STAR (Euphorbia pulcherrima) 158
    CICAS (Cycas revoluta) 159
    CISSUS ANTARCTICA (Cissus antarctica) 160
    CORK OAK (Quercus suber) 161
    CRASSULA ARBORESCENS (Crassula arborescens) 162

CRYPTOMERIA (Cryptomeria japonica) 163
DAISY (Chrysanthemum) 164
DWARF ORANGE (Fortunella hindsii) 165
ERETHIA BUXIFOLIA (Carmona microphylla) 166
EUFORBIA (Euphorbia balsamifera) 167
FERN (Grevillea robust) 168
FICUS (Retusa Ginseng) 169
FUCHSIA (Fuchsia fulgens hybrida) 171
GARDENIA (Gardenia jasminoides) 172
GINCO (Ginkgo biloba) 173
JAPANESE MAPLE (ACER PALMATUM) 174
JUBUTICABA (Myrciaria cauliflora) 176
LANTANA (Lantana camara) 177
LEBANON CEDAR (Cedrus Libani) 178
LEMON (Citrus limon) – 179
MAGNOLIA (Magnolia stellata) 180
MARJORAM (Majorana hortensis) 181
MULBERRY-TREE (Morus alba) 182
MURRAYA PANICULATA (Murraya paniculata) 183
MYRTLE CRESPO (Lagerstroemia indica) 184
NEEDLE JUNIPER (Juniperus rigida) 184
OAK (QUERCUS) 186
OLIVE (Olea europea) 188
OSMANTO (Osmanthus ilicifolius) 188
PEACH (Prunus persica) – 190
PINE (Pino silvestris) 191

PISTACHIO (Pistacia chinensis) 192
PITTOSPORUM (Pittosporum Tobira) 193
PLANTING WILLOW (Salix babylonica) 194
PODOCARPO (Podocarpus macrophylla) 195
POMEGRANATE (Punica granatum Nana) 196
QUINCE (Malus baccata) 198
ROSEMARY (Rosamrinus officinalis) 199
RUBBER FIG (Ficus microcarpa) 200
SAGEREZIA (Sagerezia theezans) 201
SCHEFFLERA (Schefflera actinophylla) 202
TEA (Carmona microphylla) 203
WEPPING WILLOW (Salix repens) 204
WHITE-FIR (Abies alba) 206

Conclusion 207
References 209
References for Images 210

© **Copyright 2021 - All rights reserved.**
The content contained within this book may not be reproduced, duplicated or transmitted without direct written permission from the author or the publisher.
Under no circumstances will any blame or legal responsibility be held against the publisher, or author, for any damages, reparation, or monetary loss due to the information contained within this book. Either directly or indirectly.

Legal Notice:
This book is copyright protected. This book is only for personal use. You cannot amend, distribute, sell, use, quote or paraphrase any part, or the content within this book, without the consent of the author or publisher.

Disclaimer Notice:
Please note the information contained within this document is for educational and entertainment purposes only. All effort has been executed to present accurate, up to date, and reliable, complete information. No warranties of any kind are declared or implied. Readers acknowledge that the author is not engaging in the rendering of legal, financial, medical or professional advice. The content within this book has been derived from various sources. Please consult a licensed professional before attempting any techniques outlined in this book.

By reading this document, the reader agrees that under no circumstances is the author responsible for any losses, direct or indirect, which are incurred as a result of the use of information contained within this document, including, but not limited to, — errors, omissions, or inaccuracies.

INTRODUCTION

Bonsai is a special art form used in Japan where live trees are grown in pots or containers. Similar practices exist in other Eastern cultures, but because of the peaceful tranquility of these practices, many of them have been adopted across the world. The term "bonsai" is a rather broad term, but directly translated it means miniature potted trees.

There are many reasons why someone would want to grow or own a bonsai. Even though it's a practice that takes a lot of patience, gentleness, and understanding, it is one of the most rewarding practices or hobbies that anyone could try. Nurturing a bonsai isn't something to be taken lightly because it does take time and effort, but those who do embark on this tranquil journey of growth and discovering peace are never disappointed.

This book is divided into different sections and even though it will take time to work through each one, all of these techniques are designed for beginners. Bonsais have increased in popularity and can be found relatively easily in large gardening stores, in specialty shops, and online. Some enthusiasts like to have trees that are already established, but you might find that you would like to grow your bonsai from a seed or seedling. The latter can be more rewarding, but it does take years of patience.

Whichever you choose, you won't be disappointed in learning how to grow, cultivate, and nurture your very own bonsai.

The term bonsai, from the Japanese *bon* (pot) and *sai* (tree), indicates an art form that allows you to grow miniature trees and plants, through meticulous daily care.

Originally, the bonsai spread to China where the skill of the masters reached the point of creating real tiny landscapes populated by mountains, rivers, houses, and people.

It is said that the poet Guen-Ming, in the fourth century after Christ, had retired to devote himself to planting and caring for chrysanthemums in some containers, thus starting the cultivation of plants in pots.

Two hundred years later, a new art was created in China, the Pen-Jin, as shown by various paintings of the Tang Dynasty (618-906), depicting dwarf trees used as ornaments.

During the 14th century, under the Ming Dynasty, bonsai were already widespread and were cultivated giving life to various styles.

However, bonsai is not only born as an aesthetic requirement but also as a spiritual exercise, as a search for harmony between man and nature, within the principles of the Zen discipline. The bonsai artist tests himself, brings his inner world closer to the outer one, trying to imprison and regulate the millennial forces of nature. In following his art, he is guided by the Zen concepts of naturalness, simplicity, harmony, and concentration on the essential.

When bonsai arrived in Japan, as a gift from wealthy Chinese, it fascinated the aristocracy precisely because of its spiritual intensity, thus becoming one of the nobility's favorite art forms. For Japan, this was the period of the spread of Zen Buddhism, during the Heian era, between the eighth and twelfth centuries.

But there is another version of the history of the Japanese art of growing bonsai.

The art of cultivating bonsais may be an ancient practice, but Japan isn't where it originally began. Bonsai cultivation was adopted from the Chinese practice of penjing, which also involves growing miniature trees in pots and small containers.

From as early as the sixth century, personnel from the Chinese Imperial Embassy and Japanese students of Buddhism traveled to mainland China where they returned with tree seedlings in potted containers as souvenirs. The Japanese students went on 17 missions to China between the years of 603 and 839 where they not only kept returning with these souvenirs, they also gained a lot of knowledge on how to cultivate them from the Tang court.

The philosophy and primary purpose of growing these trees is to bring a sense of peace and awe for the grower and anyone who gazes upon it. Once the monks started to realize how beautiful these little creations were and how pleasant it was to grow these potted trees, they instantly fell in love with the whole process. Growing bonsais was an unusual custom because plants were usually grown during those time periods to either provide food or medicine, but bonsais provided neither of these.

But the real reason for growing bonsai has a much different meaning than merely growing plants for food or medicine and has a much deeper spiritual and emotional meaning behind it.

CHAPTER 1 - THE PRINCIPLES OF BONSAI ART

The bonsai artist cultivates and takes care of his creation in a small container and trying to reproduce a glimpse of nature inside his home, which preserves the harmony of proportions, despite being significantly reduced in size.

He tries to draw its entire splendor from the plant, placing it in a landscape that resembles the real one for everything and enhancing its shape and qualities.

Like any plastic art, bonsai must also respect the basic principles of form, line, texture, space and color. The bonsai artist must always keep these concepts in mind to give value to his creation.

The form is any characteristic or structure that identifies a particular object. Even trees have their own shape, typical of the species they belong to; populate forests, woods and grasslands, adapting to the most diverse climates. Shapes and scenarios that we must strive to recreate in our bonsai.

The line establishes the border or boundary within which a work of art is created. For bonsai, limits are defined by the lines of the container, and the bonsai artist must learn to choose the suitable spatial boundaries within which to place his plant, highlighting its fundamental characteristics.

The texture is the set of structural qualities of a work of art and is born from how an artist works the chosen materials; even bonsai have their own texture, due to the structure of the leaves, the foliage, the trunk, etc.

In some compositions, therefore, some bonsai may be more appropriate than others for the characteristics of their texture: In case you want to highlight the knottiness of a trunk, for example, it is good to choose a tree with a particular bark, or if you want a contrast in the texture, you can combine deciduous trees with evergreen trees.

Space is defined, in art, as the extension that opens in all directions and in the three dimensions, within which things exist.

In bonsai, space is very important, both in the case of compositions, to establish the distance between the trees, and in the case of single trees, in order to obtain the right ratio inside container, space must, therefore, be dosed appropriately, avoiding disproportions or imbalances in the composition.

Finally, color is the sensation due to the stimulation of the retina by the light waves reflected by objects, which thus take on our eyes, particular characteristics and values.

Even bonsai have their colors, not only those of the trunk, leaves and flowers but also those dominant in the various seasons, such as the intermediate shades of the autumn and spring periods. All these elements must be taken into account during the realization of your project.

The bonsai artist must, however, also follow other rules, which allow you to set the creation and processing of any work of art. Let's talk about balance, rhythm, emphasis and unity.

The balance can be symmetrical or asymmetrical and implies certain stability of the figure. In bonsai art, however, symmetry is considered boring and therefore to be avoided. Rather, we try to give movement to the compositions and we tend to the variety of the form.

Rhythm implies a harmonious succession of the form so that the eye moves through the whole work, without interruption from start to finish.

The rhythm is very important for the bonsai that must hit the eye for its general appearance more than for some details, particularly interesting.

The emphasis gives particular relevance to a small part or to an entire area of an object. It can be obtained, either through the decision of the line, or through the specific use of color, or with lighting effects, or through the skillful use of details.

In bonsai, the emphasis can be used to highlight a feature of the plant that we particularly like, which will contribute to the movement of the composition.

Finally, the unit uses color, line, shape, texture and space to obtain a figure that satisfies us as a whole.

To achieve this, it is necessary that each of the elements mentioned completely harmonizes with the others.

By following these principles, a good bonsai artist can manage to obtain a bonsai of excellent value and remarkable value.

The whole process of growing bonsais will start off very similarly to growing any other plant or tree. An initial specimen will be introduced into the nutrient-filled source material. The specimen can be a cutting, seedling, germinating seed, or a small tree that is a suitable species for growing bonsais. Many species of trees are suitable for bonsai development and an enthusiast is able to choose from a variety of species, as long as the tree or shrub species is woody-stemmed, lives for longer than two years, is able to produce good branches, can be grown in a small pot to prune the roots.

Choosing the right type of bonsai is important because some trees are more difficult to maintain than others. Some bonsais require more sunlight than others and others may require more or less water. The best types of trees will be discussed in chapters to come, but it's important to choose a tree that you would like to tend to every day for the next several years. Even if you choose a slightly more difficult tree as a beginner, you can still successfully grow and nurture it if you give it enough time, love, and attention.

Whatever species you initially choose, especially if you are growing it from a seedling, you need to choose a bonsai that can be shaped to be relatively small throughout its lifetime and can meet all of the aesthetic standards that bonsai should meet. It's easy to grow a tree in a pot, but if it doesn't meet the aesthetic requirements of a full-grown tree, it starts to lose its point. One of the greatest visual factors of a bonsai is the fact that it looks like a miniature version of a large tree and becomes a living piece of art that you care for every day.

Because this is a piece of art, you want it to meet the specifications that you want. Of course, it is living and growing and it will change over time, but you will be able to change it according to the style that you like and you will be able to use a decorative pot that you like when you're planting your bonsai. You can choose multiple pots of different sizes as the tree grows but ensure that you choose one that is special to you to use when the tree is reaching its maximum size.

Find a place in your house that receives a fair amount of sunlight because most bonsai don't fare well with reflected light. In the Japanese tradition, it is practically unheard of to keep these trees indoors and they are usually kept outside in a protected area. But as bonsais have been adopted by more Western cultures, more people prefer to keep their bonsais indoors so they can watch them more regularly throughout the day. This makes it slightly more challenging to keep the tree healthy and it does take work, but this isn't impossible to accomplish.

The fundamental aspect of growing a bonsai is to do adequate research. As with starting any new hobby, it's necessary to find out which bonsai would be best suited to your environment, which one you like the look of, and which one you would like to nurture for years to come. The techniques that you will need to create a beautiful bonsai will all be discussed in the sections to come, but don't feel that you can't experiment with some of them.

As part of the fundamentals of growing bonsai, it is a deeply personal experience, and you can adapt certain techniques according to how you want your piece of art to grow.

The most important fundamental of bonsai growing is to love the entire process. There are going to be times that you may get frustrated or even impatient, but you will learn a lot about yourself during this process. It will help you find your inner peace if you allow it. There will be times you are going to be worried about your tree, especially when you prune the roots, but take it slow and treat it right and your bonsai will live for decades.

Before starting to describe the actual practical work, it is good to dwell a moment on some interesting distinctions that allow us to establish the first classification of bonsai.

It is important, in fact, to distinguish bonsai into two large groups:

Outdoor and indoor ones. The first are those who live in the open air without any particular damage.

They usually belong to species accustomed to climates characterized by significant changes in temperature and sudden changes of season.

The latter, however, are those that need a moderate and constant temperature to survive. To these belong many tropical and subtropical species, such as ficus, schefflera, jacaranda, which would live very little if left exposed to our climates. Therefore, it is always good to read up on the needs and climatic habits of the plant, so as to offer it the best possible living condition.

Bonsai trees are also classified according to their height, which can vary from a minimum of 6 inches to a maximum of 47 inches. The "miniature" bonsai do not exceed the height of 6 inches.

The "small" bonsai is less than 8.6 inches in size and are more readily available on the market. The "medium-small" bonsai reach the height of 16inches and for this, they are more easily cultivated. Then there are the "medium" bonsai that vary between 16 inches and 35 inches and the "large" ones, with a maximum height of 47 inches.

CHAPTER 2 - HOW TO GROW BONSAI

Those who are about to undertake the art of bonsai must keep in mind that it is a job that requires great attention and considerable patience, along with all the stages of development and growth of your bonsai, from the first moment of cutting the roots, the choice of the pot, the shape that the bonsai will have to take.

The beginner will not be able to immediately breed an excellent quality bonsai, but he will still be able to achieve many satisfactions managing to keep the size of the chosen tree or plant considerably reduced. The starting point of the work concerns the choice between the various ways to obtain a bonsai plant that meets our needs and abilities.

There are multiple ways that bonsai can be cultivated and some techniques are slightly more complicated than others, but given the right time and patience, all of these techniques can be performed by beginner enthusiasts. You might want to try your hand at a few of these methods once you fall in love with the whole process, but you may want to pick one of these methods first and then try it out.

There are many ways to get a map that can serve our purposes; among the most common, we will remember: Bonsai taken in nature, grown from seed, multiplied by cutting, multiplied by layering, obtained by grafting, bonsai purchased in a nursery. In this order, the main rules to be observed for the best results will be listed.

In this order, the main rules to be observed for best results will be listed.

Once you're confident with that method, move onto the next. This is a continuous learning process and you will discover something new about these little pieces of art every time you work with them.

RECOVERED IN NATURE OR YAMADORI

The Japanese translation for Yamadori means to collect small trees from a wild place like a forest. Sometimes trees can naturally remain small in nature because of a lack of sunlight, water, or nutrients in the soil. If two trees, for example, grow right next to each other, one's roots might grow faster and deeper allowing it to absorb more nutrients and water than its neighbor. This will allow its leaves and foliage to develop more quickly and it will start absorbing more sunlight. This will cast a shadow over its neighbor and then stunt its growth.

A rather easy way to get a plant is to take it directly in its natural environment: Going into a forest, it is often easy to find small plants that can meet our needs, requiring only the time of the pleasant walk.

Japan many bonsai, among the most famous for their beauty and seniority, like many black pines with five needles or junipers, were obtained with the Yamadori method.

However, not all the plants we encounter are suitable for becoming a bonsai, because, for various reasons, they would not grow in the right way, disappointing our expectations.

One of the best places to look in the wild for small trees that are advanced in years but still small in stature is close to larger trees that cast a shadow on them. Although it can be rather difficult to successfully dig out a small tree from the wild without over-damaging its root structure, these are the trees with some of the greatest and most unique bonsai properties. But digging up a tree may be illegal, so if this is something you want to do, you will need to first ascertain whether it is legal in that area and possibly get permission from the owner of the land.

The first thing to do, therefore, is to consider only plants that show themselves as the most robust and healthy, with small leaves, uniformly arranged on the branches.

It is good to make sure that the roots are also strong and well developed, and that the branches have grown in many directions, to give an impression of movement. Overall, the plant should look strong, small but compact.

Once the plant is chosen, the most delicate phase is that of transplanting, so it is good to pay close attention to how the operation is performed. The recommended period is just before spring when the vegetation awakens and the climate softens.

The roots defend themselves better from damage and are more willing to take root easily in new soil. However, good results were also achieved in late spring, between April and May, especially in mountain areas, and in autumn. Here's how it goes.

If you know that it's legal and you have the required permission, it's best to go out in the early months of spring to find a tree to dig up. Once you have found the tree that you think will make a suitable bonsai, then you should start digging around the tree carefully.

The soil around the tree is cleaned of blades of grass that hinder the work and those branches that will not serve our purpose or those that have grown excessively in length are cut, making the plant more manageable.

Dig a foot radius around the whole tree and also dig approximately a foot into the earth. It's important to take care that you don't overly damage the roots when you're digging. Ensure that when you cut through the roots, you do it as cleanly as possible, because roots that are overly bent and damaged will struggle to re-establish themselves later on and the tree will take the strain in its container.

Once the roots have carefully been severed, remove the tree from the earth and wrap the roots and remaining soil in moist towels to protect the roots while transportation. If the roots dry out, the tree will eventually die, so this is a necessary step and mustn't be skipped. It's important to note that the tree will be under stress while it's being transported and needs to be placed in a pot and re-soiled as soon as possible.

Any potting soil will suffice, but it must be nutrient-rich, so compost or diluted fertilizer should be included in the soil to help the roots after their trauma. If possible, it is ideal to include as much soil that the tree originally grew in into the pot because it's soil that the tree and the roots are already used to. This can be mixed in accordingly.

When preparing the pot, you need to use one that can drain well. A bonsai that receives too much water and can't get rid of the excess will not fare very well and may even die prematurely. Fill the pot with a mixture of soil and gravel to ensure adequate drainage and space for the roots to fit and grow into the container comfortably. (When making the soil mixture, ensure you use 50% soil and 50% gravel.)

If the plant is to be transported, the earth is sprayed with water and wrapped with damp gauze or newsprint, tying everything with twine in order to facilitate transport. It can be convenient to place the plant in a nylon bag that will also allow you to keep humidity constant. For a couple of months, waiting for the plant to resume all its functions, it is good to keep it in a normal pot with unfertilized soil, watering it abundantly and keeping it sheltered from wind and sun.

A perforated transparent plastic bell is recommended to limit evaporation. When it begins to throw the first shoots, then you can proceed with the repotting in a bonsai container.

Finally, gently unwrap the root system of the tree from the moist towel and place it in the pot. Once all of the roots are moved gently and comfortably placed, cover the soil/gravel mixture of the roots and pat down gently. It's best not to have the earth compacted because it will affect watering the roots.

Once the tree is securely planted, gently water it so as not to disturb the soil and the settling roots. The tree would be at risk at this point because its roots were damaged, so gentle care will be needed in the beginning stages. Watering heavily could disrupt the settling roots and harm the tree. After the bonsai has been watered, place it outside in a highly lit area, but keep it out of direct sunlight. A tree of this size probably isn't used to direct sunlight and it will dry out the soil much more quickly.

Keep the soil damp but never drenched, and leave the tree practically untouched for an entire year. If the bonsai is thriving after a year, then you can start styling it and considering repotting it if you need to. Additionally, it's necessary to occasionally include diluted fertilizers during the first year and especially in the summer months. The combination of warmth and nutrients will help the roots thrive. This will establish the tree and keep it healthy for years to come.

CULTIVATION FROM SEED OR MISHO

If you are the type of person who loves to start things from the very beginning and if you have the patience to enjoy this entire process, then the Misho method will be very satisfying.

This is the decidedly more fascinating method as it allows the seedling to grow and to follow its development from its seed state; however, it is also the method that takes the longest time before truly embarking on the art of bonsai. Sometimes there is talk of several years.

This method involves growing your bonsai from a tree seed of your choice and although it does take a very long time, you have a hands-on experience with the entire process.

It will take a minimum of three years for a seedling to be mature enough to actually start shaping it into what you desire, but it does put you at an advantage because you have full control over your bonsai from the very beginning.

If this is the route that you would like to take, then there are several places where you can get tree seeds suitable for growing a bonsai. You can look in your surroundings or you can shop for some online. Do keep in mind that since bonsais are normal trees, they will come from normal tree seeds. There is no such thing as bonsai seeds and some people will try and sell these "bonsai tree seeds" at a much more expensive price, where in reality you could have probably found them outside for free.

If you do choose to look in your surroundings for tree seeds, then your future bonsai will be at an immediate advantage because if those types of trees are growing naturally in your area, then you are already in the perfect environment and climate for your bonsai to thrive.

Any locally sourced seeds should be planted as soon as fall begins for the best possible results. If you are interested in growing a foreign bonsai, it will be necessary to research exactly when it will be the best time to plant the seeds. If you are interested in planting seeds that come from a different region with a different climate, then you may need to employ a stratification technique to germinate the seeds.

The seeds can be found directly in nature, which implies a good one seed knowledge or purchased from a dealer. In both cases, it is important to bear in mind that some seeds need special care before they can be planted.

Some species must be subjected to a pre-germination period in which the seeds are left for 24 hours in a basin full of water, the fertile seeds will deposit on the bottom forfeiting water, and the others will remain on the surface.

Other species must spend a cool period, between 2 and 8 degrees Celsius - 46.4 F., to be able to mature. In any case, it would be good to seek advice from a gardener who can adequately inform us about the needs of the various species of seeds.

As for seeds to buy, the packs on which the word Bonsai is written are preferred, even if any seed can become a good bonsai. But now, let's continue the job description.

After making the first decisions on the choice of seed, proceed with sowing.

The Stratification Technique

Stratification is the process of allowing seeds to germinate by simulating their natural growing conditions. Many tree seeds have the genetic programming to survive through the cold winter months in the ground and then start germinating in the spring. This enables them to maximize their chances of successfully growing into a tree and many tree seeds are only able to germinate after they've gone through a cold winter period.

Therefore, if you are planting tree seeds out of season or from different climates, it may be needed to simulate a cold season to increase the likelihood of the seeds germinating. The majority of tree species will require you to soak the seeds in water before storing them in the refrigerator for a couple of months.   Some   seeds require less time in a cold climate, whereas other species may require up to three months in the cold, so it will be necessary to research this before you begin the stratification process.

Planting the Seeds

The seedbed consisting of a small container filled with poor soil, which is without fertilizers (usually a mixture of sand and peat), is prepared. In this state, the seed is already in itself wrapped in sufficient nutrients to allow it to develop well.

The container should be filled up to 2 inches from the edge.

The initial preparation of your pot or container will be exactly the same for planting seeds as it would be for planting cuttings or a small tree. You will first apply a layer of coarse ground like gravel or lava rock at the bottom of the container to allow for adequate drainage. If seeds sit in soil that is too wet, it will cause them to rot and they won't be able to sprout.

Once you have added the soil layer on top of the coarse layer, you can start preparing your seeds. If your seeds need to be stratified, do this first, but if you have sourced local seeds and you are planting them at the right time, then you can forgo this process.

Once the moment of sowing has arrived (usually spring), proceed by burying the seeds with light pressure, the larger ones must be covered by at least 1inch of soil, the smaller ones by 0.5 inch.

If the size of the seed is really tiny then it will be sufficient to spread it regularly. We then begin to water them abundantly and gently, taking care not to create harmful grooves in the ground.

A solution with Chinosol can also be used.

Place the seeds in a container but ensure you leave at least two inches of space between each one. As the seeds continue to grow, they will require extra space for their roots to spread. And, if the roots intertwine you may end up damaging them when you try to re-pot the individual shoots. This can hurt the bonsai's progress.

Once the seeds are planted, another inch of bonsai soil must be added on top of the seeds and then gently compacted with your fingers. Once this is completed, water thoroughly and allow to drain. After that, don't water heavily again and only keep the soil moist until the seeds start to sprout.

Leave the seedlings alone for a year before you consider repotting. Performing this too early can put unnecessary strain on the root systems of the seedlings. Once they have been repotted, you must wait for at least another year before you consider shaping the bonsai. Even though this is a long process, it is still very satisfying to watch the little trees take form over this time.

At this point, it would be useful to cover the container with a glass or plastic bell, so as to keep the soil at a certain humidity and temperature (the ideal one is 18-20 degrees Celsius - 64.4-68 F.).

The container should be kept away from the sun, often watering the soil to prevent the seeds from drying out.

For this operation, the use of an inclined onion or a nebulizer is recommended, because, if the jet were too strong, it would move the earth and make the seeds float.

Once the seedlings are born, the bell can be removed and when the first leaves have sprouted, the transplant is carried out in a new container. It is important not to fertilize the land for at least a month.

After this period, the fertilizer will be administered in half the dose compared to that written on the pack.

When the height of the seedlings will be 4 inches, you can begin to act on the shape.

MULTIPLICATION BY CUTTINGS OR SASHIKI

This method Sashiki consists of obtaining a new seedling using a part of an already formed plant. This allows us two main advantages: First, we can easily dispose of a lot of bonsai material, simply by removing the parts of the plant that interest us.

Secondly, the multiplication by cutting allows us to maintain the same characteristics typical of the mother plant with absolute fidelity also for the following generations.

However, even the cutting method while very easy to implement, is time-consuming. The cuttings are divided into four groups: It is possible to obtain a stem cutting, a sprouting cutting, a leaf-cutting and a root cutting.

The Sashiki method is one of the most popular and inexpensive ways for bonsai enthusiasts to propagate new trees because this process involves using tree cuttings. This method is much faster than trying to grow new trees through germinating seeds, and by using cuttings, the bonsai enthusiast can have more of an indication of some of the characteristics that the cutting will have if it starts to grow.

It is best to plan to gather tree cuttings in the spring and summer months when the trees are vibrant. Once you have decided which cuttings you would like (deciduous and conifer trees are normally the most successful), start gathering several cuttings. Look for healthy trees with healthy branches and make each cutting between two and four inches long. Additionally, look for branches that are only around an eighth of an inch thick, because they have greater success rates than thicker branches.

It's important to gather several cuttings at once because there is no guarantee that all of them will take root. Some of them may not be successful and if you only have one specimen, you may feel disheartened if it fails. But, if you have several specimens, the chances are greatly increased that one, or a few of them, will take root.

To ensure that the cuttings sprout roots, it's imperative to plant them in a substrate that will assist this process. In a small pot that can drain readily and easily, pour in a layer of a coarse draining substrate like gravel or lava rock. This substrate has no nutrients, but it helps the water drain far more quickly. Fill the container to around ⅓ of the way and then add a layer of bonsai soil. (Bonsai soil can be purchased at gardening shops and online and has a fair amount of nutrients, more than regular potting soil.)

But now we describe the simpler methods adopted:

Stem cutting: The stem cutting, also called eda-zashi, uses already fully mature and robust branches. These, if buried or immersed in water, develop their own root system, becoming autonomous plants.

Therefore, branches not older than three years and which are not perishable due to disease or insects are to be chosen.

Prune the cuttings at a 45-degree angle and place them into the soil about an inch deep. Once all of the cuttings are pushed into the soil, water the soil well and allow it to drain before putting it in a well-lit 45-degree area. After the initial heavy watering, keep the water moist and don't allow it to dry out. The nutrients from the soil will help the cuttings sprout roots and most should be successful.

The branch must be around 8 inches long and must be cut immediately under a leaf node. The sprig must then be cleaned from the base by the leaves and planted in the ground, making sure that the shoots remain on the surface as much as needed.

After the cuttings have sprouted, plant them in individual little containers and allow them to grow. Cuttings are very successful ways of growing bonsais, but it will take several years before you will be able to shape them according to what you would like. But it's worth it and you won't be disappointed with this method.

It must then be watered abundantly and covered with a glass or plastic plate.

It is important that during the first months the pot is in a bright place without being exposed to direct sun and that the soil is kept constantly humid. Once the first roots have sprouted, the seedling can be discovered from the slab and fertilized.

Transplanting into a bonsai container should only be done once the roots are fully formed to develop.

Cutting from shoots: The cutting from shoots, called shinme-zashi, uses a young shoot to develop a new plant.

The shoot must be cut obliquely with a sharp blade and must be leafless in the lowest part of its length. The other leaves, on the other hand, are simply to be checked by a third, so that evaporation is reduced to a minimum. Then the leafless stem of the bud is wrapped with a clay ball with a diameter of 1 inch, making sure that the lower part of the bud is positioned approximately in the center of the clay ball. You can finally proceed to bury the sprout up to completely cover the part wrapped in clay.

Leaf-cutting: Leaf-cutting, or ha-zashi, consists of planting a sprig in the soil leaving a leaf on the surface. The soil must be watered carefully and kept away from the sun. The sprig will emit the roots and develop other leaves.

Root cutting: The root cutting, called ne-zashi, consists instead of gathering the roots of the chosen tree during the winter season and cutting them into 3 inches long pieces. A container should be prepared to contain damp sand, on which the roots will be placed and left to rest until spring. Important, to cover the container with a glass plate and leave it at a temperature of 2-4 degrees Celsius – 35,6-39,2 F..

When the roots begin to develop, transplanting can be carried out in suitable soil, making sure that the outermost part of the root is at ground level.

SPROUT CUTTING

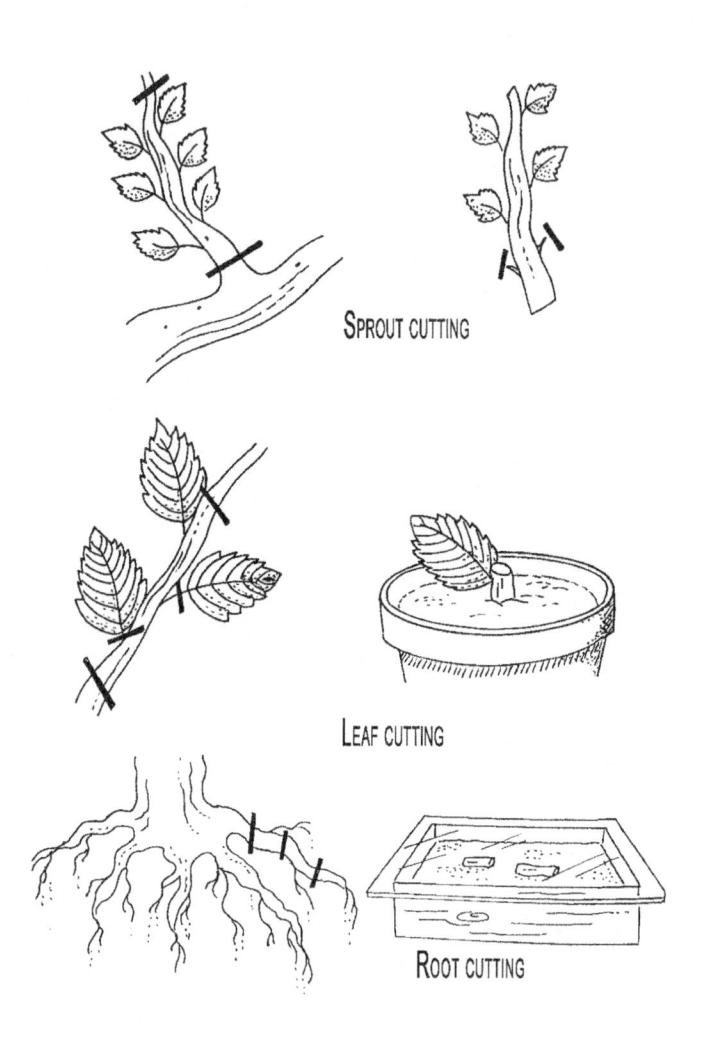

LEAF CUTTING

ROOT CUTTING

MULTIPLICATION BY LAYERING OR TORIKI

This method of cultivating bonsais is slightly more challenging but it can still be performed by a beginner if they are up to a challenge.

The Toriki method works with air-layering and this allows for a tree or a branch of a tree to start forming new roots at a higher level because the nutrients of the existing root system have been interrupted. This sounds confusing, but sometimes a tree's trunk starts dividing into two, allowing two separate branches to grow.

Air-layering should always be done in the spring so the roots aren't exposed to extremes in temperatures and spring also maximizes the chances of roots sprouting.

This multiplication by layering consists of putting in contact a branch of the plant specially engraved with peat or earth, to make it root.

This is a method that allows you to obtain seedlings from rather large branches, in a short time, which would instead be very difficult to achieve by cutting.

The layering is recommended above all on some types of plants such as the Pomegranate, the Spruce, the Myrtle, the Maple, the Elm and the Cryptomeria, which have a great ability to develop roots both from the trunk and from the branches.

It is preferable to undertake the operation in the spring, even if good results are obtained at any time of the year. Let's see how it goes together.

There are two different methods that can be used to air-layer a tree, namely the tourniquet method and the ring method. These methods are only used on trunks that are bifurcated and one that an enthusiast can remove one of the sections and grow a new bonsai from it.

The Ring: If you are more confident and believe that you will be able to grow the roots more quickly and cut away some bark without hurting the tree, the ring method may prove to be very successful.

Once the branch of the plant has been chosen, the lateral jets are removed for a short distance and engraved in the bark, forming a ring of about 1 inch in height around which the roots will form.

Two cuts from the bottom up to the sides of the branch can also be practiced, introducing a pebble or peat into the wound so that it does not close again.

There is also a third method of practicing the wound, consisting of wrapping two very close circles of wire tightly in the established point. In this way, with the growth of the tree, the wire will cut the bark gradually.

It is also important to sprinkle the wound with rooting hormone powder and prevent it from healing.

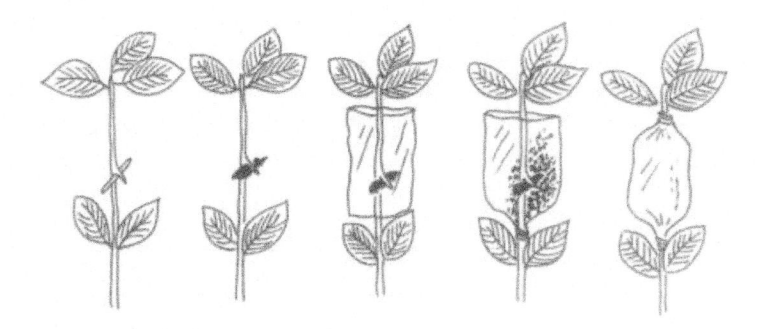

Layering Procedure

To obtain the roots, a transparent polyethylene sleeve stops under the incision, so as to create a funnel, and it is filled with peat to wrap the wound.

The sleeve is also closed over the incision with adhesive tape and the peat is constantly moistened. If the operation is unsuccessful, the branch will wither and die after a week or two; otherwise, the roots will begin to sprout.

When the root system is thick enough (usually 6-8 weeks), the new plant can be cut under the incision, placing it definitively in a container.

When the roots have well-rooted in the pot, you can proceed with the development of the bonsai.

Trees can be quite stubborn and they won't start sprouting roots until they are forced to do so. Thus, cutting a significant ring in the bark and including root hormone will force the tree to start sprouting roots in a place where it normally wouldn't. Once the wound has been dusted with root hormone, wrap it in wet sphagnum moss and then in plastic.

The Tourniquet: It's going to take some time and preparation to be confident enough to perform this method, but the first step is to wrap a piece of copper wire very tightly around the segment that you would like to cut off from the main trunk (preferably on one of the smaller off-shoots.) You should be able to use normal copper wire for this process, but if you have a bonsai with a thick trunk or a tree with a thick type of bark, you may need to use a copper wire with a thicker circumference.

Once you have tied the wire around the segment, it's important to sprinkle some rooting hormone over the damaged bark. This hormone, along with the lack of nutrients in the trunk, will cause roots to sprout quickly because the tree is going to try and survive the trauma. After the rooting hormone is added to the wound around the wire, wrap it with wet sphagnum moss and wrap it with plastic.

This method is less extreme than the ring method because it doesn't damage the bark as severely as the ring method but it does still sprout roots fairly quickly.

The Care for These Methods: Once the moss has been tied with plastic around the wounds, it is necessary to keep the moss moist at all times. It isn't advised to drench the moss because it will hinder the root growth, but keeping it moist will accelerate the growth of the roots. It will take a few months for the bag to fill with roots, but keep the stem attached to the main trunk during this process. Only when the bag is completely filled should you remove the stem with gentle cuts and plant the roots into fertile bonsai soil.

This method is tricky, but because you can remove a section of a bonsai that is already established, you will find that this will allow for rapid growth afterward; instead of waiting four or five years before you can start shaping the tree, it may be possible to start shaping the tree in around half the time.

PROPAGATION BY GRAFTING OR TSUGIKI

The Tsugiki method is also one of the more advanced methods and will take some practice, but just like the Toriki method, this method is also very rewarding. Translated from Japanese, Tsugiki means "to graft," and just like most other plant species, bonsais do thrive well with grafts.

Grafting two plants or trees together allows the strengths and characteristics of both plants to come through in their future development. This usually is beneficial to produce tastier fruits or more resilient plants, but grafting helps to add branches where needed and increase the foliage on a certain part of the tree. Some enthusiasts also try to combine the characteristics of two different trees that they like into one bonsai, but grafting is not an easy process and it can be risky. Without adequate practice, most grafts may be unsuccessful, so it's imperative to practice this technique on much cheaper plants and trees before you try it on a costly bonsai.

One of the most important principles of grafting is that you have to graft two trees between the same or a very similar species. Trees that are two different won't be compatible and the graft won't take. This won't only kill the graft, it might irreversibly damage the tree too. If you want to add to your bonsai, then you need to graft in branches of a species that is part of the same class or subclass.

Grafting is another way to get a bonsai plant. It consists of joining two different plants, to add their qualities into one. The plant on which the graft is practiced takes the name of "subject" or "portliness" (daiki), while the branch that is grafted is called "scion" or "grafting" (sugan: This process can be very useful for aesthetic purposes, to protect the plant from particular parasites, or to obtain a greater variety of fruit). In bonsai art, however, this method is often not recommended, especially the two types of grafting: A) *Basic grafting;* B) *Top grafting to* beginners, due to the special care and experience it requires.

The grafting is generally practiced during the spring and with very young trees, of two or three years, which manage to adapt more easily to the various situations.

Now let's see how the two main types of grafting are made: The top ones and the base ones.

Top graft: Also called ten-tsugi or Scion grafting, is made in the upper part of a plant. It is the most common sort of grafting, and it involves removing a small branch or shoot from a larger donor plant and then inserting it into another plant. With this type of graft, the end of the shoot is cut at a 45-degree angle and then a similar groove is made into the receiving plant, so the shoot can fit snugly into the groove.

This technique is commonly used with juniper and pine trees, but most deciduous and evergreen trees cope very well with this type of grafting. If you have a bonsai of one of these species, you can use this grafting method to easily add extra branches or include extra foliage on the top of the tree. (The leaves on top of bonsais can seem rather sparse, so this is a way to make your bonsai seem fuller and allow for a richer look.) When these grafts are done carefully and they fit well in the beginning, there will be a little-to-no indication that there ever was a graft performed.

It is absolutely necessary to ensure that both the donor and the receiver are both in good health. If one of the trees is in ill health, the graft won't be successful, and if there is an infection in the graft, there is a small risk of spreading it to the receiving tree. Always ensure that both trees have healthy foliage and seem very similar in stature before grafting. One of the best ways to ensure that both trees are healthy is to fertilize both trees well in the season before you are going to graft. Since grafting is best performed in early spring, it's best to fertilize regularly throughout the spring and summer months the year prior.

It's also best to protect both trees during the winter months. Frost and snow (if you are working with larger trees) can severely damage the branches and make them less likely to be grafted together. Thus, it's best to cover the branches that you want to use for grafting (it might not be possible to cover the whole tree if the tree is large, but it is possible with most bonsais).

Once you're ready to start grafting in early spring, identify which shoots you believe are most likely to join with each other. It's ideal to look for shoots that have a strong woody base and are at least 2 ½ to 4 inches long and around a ¼ inch in diameter. Don't look for any branches that are too thick because the thinner ones have a more flexible interior and have a higher probability of joining properly.

It's necessary to clean a sharp grafting knife with alcohol before cutting a shoot from the donor tree and then re-cleaning the knife before making the groove into the receiver. It may seem strange to go to this extent, but sterilizing the blade with alcohol lowers the risk of any parasites being spread between the trees.

Cut the scion with one long stroke at an angle to create a sharp point to move into the groove of the receiving tree. Since you have gone through the trouble of cleaning your knife, do not touch the cut end of the shoot with your bare hands. Contaminating the end can lessen the likelihood of acceptance.

Once you place the shoot into the receiving tree (do this as smoothly as possible as not to hurt the wood), use grafting tape to secure the branch. Wrap it around the area that you have cut and treat it like you would treat an injury on a person. Don't tie the tape too tightly because it can cut off the nutrients into the branch, but don't leave it too loose because it comes undone and the branch may not stay secured.

Ensure that the wrapping is sufficient enough to prevent water from seeping into the graft. Unlike other planting methods, you want to avoid having water seep into any graft because it can create the shoots and the scions to start to rot. You can add some plastic wrap around the tape to help with this if you are concerned about moisture or rain.

Leave the dressing on the graft throughout the winter months and watch for any new signs of life in the spring. Any new sprouts, shoots, or flowers are indicative that the graft was successful. If you see that this is starting to occur, you can slowly unwrap the dressing around the graft because the tree would have healed at this point.

Basic graft. The basic graft, or moto-tsugi, concerns instead a lateral union that is practiced at the base of the trunk or branch of a plant.

In this case, we proceed in a slightly different way: The cut of the rootstock must be practiced literally from top to bottom for the depth of about 1 inch, creating a sort of notch in the trunk.

The cut of the scion must then be studied in an appropriate way to this notch, so as to fit perfectly into the rootstock, allowing quick healing of the wound.

Also, in this case, a strong binding will be necessary to facilitate the union of the two parts. Before transplanting it is good to cut the leaves in half and cut the main root.

This will assist in welding, limiting the growth of the rootstock.

Once practiced any of the two grafts it is good to place the plant in a place sheltered from the sun and drafts, watering to keep the soil moist, but without exceeding, so as not to rot the roots. After a month, the graft should begin to throw new shoots, then the binding must be eliminated and the soil fertilized in small doses.

However, the following factors should always be kept in mind.

Plants must be compatible: It is not possible to graft two plants that have too different characteristics, such as an apple tree and an orange.

The part of the two plants that come into contact, called the change, must be carefully joined because nourishment passes from it to the upper plant. Never practice grafting in an unsuitable season, such as winter.

The direction of the buds of the scion must be the same as that of the rootstock, i.e., upwards.

A bonsai obtained by grafting, however, can begin to show good results only after a couple of years of careful care.

NURSERY BONSAI

Buying the plant in a nursery is certainly the easiest way to start a bonsai, as it does not involve any of the risks mentioned above.

However, it excludes the great satisfaction of growing a bonsai from the early stages. It is very important, however, to carefully consider the plant you want to buy; it is easy, to come across rather expensive specimens that deserve careful consideration.

In order not to incur unpleasant accidents, we list the three main evaluation criteria of a bonsai, so that we can get an idea of the appropriate price:

The first characteristic is the age: The older a bonsai is, the higher its price will rise. However, it is well known that age is often increased during the purchase phase.

We recommend giving importance to age, but above all to focus on the aesthetic aspect of the plant we want to buy.

The general aspect of the bonsai is also important and must be healthy and vigorous.

During the purchase, therefore, it is necessary to consider the state of health and robustness of the tree, starting from the root system which must have well-developed rootlets, up to the branches and crown which must be proportionate and harmonious.

In this regard, it is good to know that if the bonsai has visible wounds; these do not diminish the value of the plant.

The important thing is that they are well healed and that they do not aesthetically ruin the general appearance.

The bonsai must have a simple shape, which respects the basic styles of which we will talk shortly.

It is therefore advisable to decide to buy the tree when you already have in mind the main characteristics that you want in bonsai, according to the style and species you have chosen.

Considering these criteria, we will be able to assess whether or not the price of a bonsai corresponds to its main characteristics.

HOW TO ATTACH BONSAI TO YOUR CONTAINER

Given the size and small thickness of many bonsai containers, there is often the risk that the plant will not be able to stand alone. It is therefore necessary to anchor it to have greater support.

There are two anchoring methods: The roots of the tree are stopped using metal wire at the bottom of the container.

This can be done in two ways: Either by tying the wire to the drainage metal mesh or by letting the wire come out of the drain hole and then stopping it under the pot.

In the case of group bonsai, only the largest trees will be anchored to the container, then tying to those smaller ones. Threads will be removed when the roots have developed sufficiently.

On the one hand, a moist mixture of potting soil and peat is prepared and wrapped, compressing it, around the roots of the tree, to weigh it down and make it more stable. It then ends by filling the container with normal soil.

We will now deal with that part of the bonsai care that concerns transplanting, that is moving the plant from one soil to another, and repotting, that is, moving from one container to another,

Transplanting has the utility of providing new fertile soil and chemical balanced to the plant.

The earth is gradually depleted by the tree that uses mineral substances as nourishment. It is therefore necessary to replace it with new soil to prevent the plant from weakening or wasting.

The main purpose of the repotting instead is to limit the size of the roots, favoring the development of rootlets which, although small in size, provide most of the nourishment to the plant.

For each repotting, therefore, you can use a smaller pot, or at the maximum keep the size of the previous pot. However, it is good to prepare the container, sterilizing it from germs, and cover it.

I give the drainage holes with a thin mesh metal mesh, so as to allow the water to pass without the soil coming out.

If the container is very high, a drainage layer of about 1inch must be created using pebbles.

This will allow the water not to stagnate. It should be remembered that the right period for repotting is the beginning of spring, except for tropical and subtropical plants which can be repotted at any time of the year.

Besides, young plants must be repotted every year, to accompany their rapid growth, while the older ones can wait even two or three years. It is however good to note that the plant needs repotting when the soil rises above the edge of the container due to the thrust that the roots provide. Repotting should be started when the soil is dry, so you can work more easily. Here's how it goes.

You turn the pot upside down and, holding the bonsai by the trunk, hit the bottom of the container so as to gently let the soil out with the roots.

After bringing the bonsai back in the right direction, proceed to clean the roots of the residual earth and shorten those too long by a third. The main root, the larger one, will be checked and dead or too weak roots will be eliminated.

After pruning, the container is filled with a thin layer of soil and the bonsai is placed in the pot, taking the measures for a correct arrangement: The root of the roots must not exceed the edge of the pot.

Pour more soil into the container without exceeding, pressing it to make it adhere well to the root system, and proceed with watering, taking care not to create grooves in the ground, and placing the pot in a sheltered place.

However, it is recommended not to use the fertilizer for at least one or two months after repotting.

It is good now to spend a few words about the ideal soil for bonsai, so as to provide each plant with the best nutritional intake and the best possibility of development.

The most suitable soil is absolutely the original one of the plants, although none is always easy to dispose of.

Therefore, different types of soil must be purchased to have a suitable mixture.

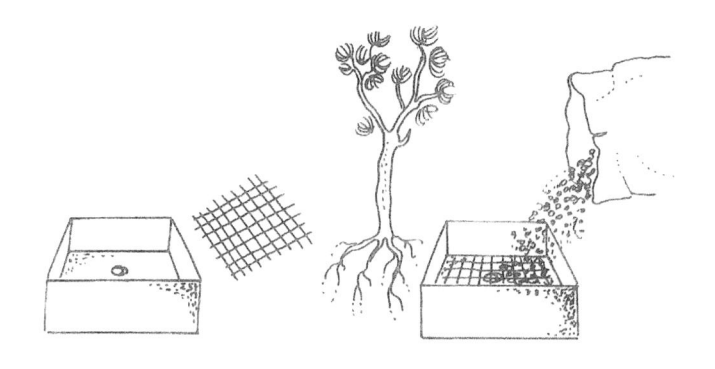

Application of metal mesh for drainage

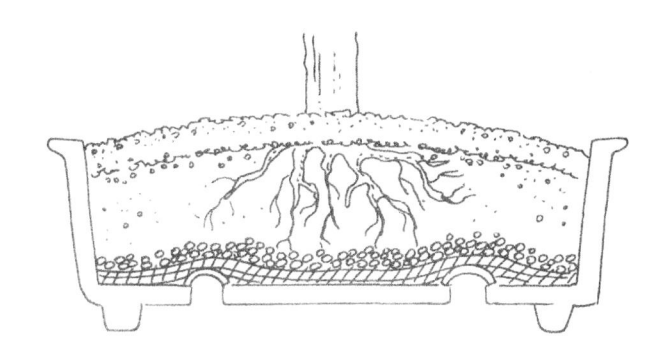

Drainage in a tall container with wire mesh and pebbles

In case you already have available the earth and you run the risk that contains insect eggs, you will have to spread it in the sun so that the eggs die.

You can also sterilize the earth with fingers or chloropicrin.

Bonsai soil is a mixture of various elements, such as peat, sand and clay. Each of these elements gives the soil certain characteristics, the clay is the actual greasy soil, and the peat provides the humus while the sand allows the soil to breathe more easily and chooses water.

However, each plant has certain needs, due to the speed of growth, the need for humidity, and above all the degree of acidity of the soil.

Acidity is a very important element for the good development of the plant, therefore, it must be carefully observed. We recommend the purchase of a pH-meter, of the mixture, so as to offer the best soil to the plant.

A large quantity of plants prefers an acidity degree between 5.5 and 6 on the pH meter scale.

We can schematize the degree of acidity necessary for the various plants in this way: Device for measuring acidity;

- PH less than 3.7: Plants that grow in areas with acidic soil.
- PH between 3.8 and 4.5: Spruce, Canadian fir, birch and poplar.
- PH between 4.6 and 5.5: Most conifers.
- PH between 5.6 and 6.9: Almost all deciduous trees.
- PH between 7.0 and 8.0: Plants that live in neutral or alkaline grasslands.

If there are imbalances between the plant and the soil, the mixture must be modified, adding a lot of peat, a very acidic substance, if we want to increase the acidity degree, or removing it, if we want to decrease it, possibly adding lime or calcium carbonate, so as to correct it further.

However, general rules can be laid down on the composition of the mixture for some plants. For example, young plants, or in general deciduous that have rather rapid growth, need more oily soil, therefore a mixture consisting of 1/3 of clay, 1/3 of peat, and 1/3 0 sand is recommended. Slow-growing plants, like conifers, need more sandy soil, so the mixture should be 1/4 clay, 1/4 peat 2/4 sand. However, it is good to sift the final mixture in order to and the soil agglomerates, making it uniform and homogeneous.

After filling the container, it is good practice to also apply the last layer of pulverized moss or leaf soil mixed with soil to give a more natural and wilder image to the creation

It is absolutely necessary to change your bonsai's pot every few years, because if a bonsai becomes pot--bound, it will deplete all the nutrients in the soil, and it will inevitably die. A tree that doesn't have its pot changed can't allow its roots to grow further, and the growth will be completely stunted. Transplanting and repotting your bonsai allows it more space and nutrients to grow and flourish.

Even though it's necessary to repot your bonsai, it won't be a regular occurrence. Even the fastest-growing trees are only repotted every couple of years and more mature trees are only repotted every three to five years. Repotting isn't something that is routine and it is something that you can judge subjectively according to your tree. You can judge this by gently removing your tree from its pot in the early months of spring and see if there are roots encircling the entire root system. If this is the case, then the bonsai needs to be repotted into a larger container before the roots strangle themselves.

The best time to repot your bonsai is in early spring because the tree is still dormant after the winter months. This is important because the tree isn't supporting foliage at this point, so if any roots are accidentally damaged during the transfer, it shouldn't cause any permanent or severe problems with your bonsai.

You can choose any style of pot for your bonsai, as long as it's large enough to comfortably house all the roots.

For this topic we have written a separate chapter in order to choose the best vase also for aesthetic reasons.

Before you repot your bonsai, ensure that you have all the necessary tools for a smooth transfer. The tools you will need for this process are a small root rake, sharp scissors for pruning, a chopstick, and a wire cutter.

If you have bought a bonsai that is already grown and potted, many sellers will anchor the tree to the pot they're planted in, and it will be necessary to cut the anchoring wire at the drainage holes to prevent you from hurting your tree when you try to remove it.

Once this is completed, carefully lift the entire ground and root mixture out of the pot using the root rake and check the root development within the pot. If the roots are still sparse and not encircling each other, you can return the tree to its original pot for another year and recheck it the following spring, but if you notice the roots are becoming cramped in the small pot, then it will be time to repot your bonsai.

Before moving the tree to its new pot, take the time to scrape away the old soil from the roots with a chopstick. This will allow new, nutrient-filled soil to take up that space to feed the bonsai in the new pot. Try your best not to damage the roots during this process, so don't rush cleaning the roots. It is important to note that if you have a pine bonsai that you chose to grow, you must keep at least half of the old soil attached to the roots because the roots grow mycorrhizal fungus and this helps nourish and protect the tree.

After you have removed the adequate amount of dirt from the roots, grab your scissors and start pruning any roots that have grown too long, but don't ever prune more than 30% of the total roots. This will cause too much trauma to the tree and the tree will have a high likelihood of dying. So, proceed with caution with this step.

Build your new pot with fine mesh over the drainage holes and fill it with the usual drainage mix and then some bonsai soil before adding the tree. Top it up with more bonsai soil until the pot is filled and press the soil down gently with your fingers. You can add a few pebbles on the top of the soil because it helps guide water and it improves the decoration of the piece itself.

Finally, water the tree thoroughly and then keep the soil moist thereafter.

CHAPTER 3 - BONSAI AND ITS STYLES

Since bonsais are living works of art and because no tree is going to grow quite like another, they all have unique traits, and these traits can be manipulated according to what you would like your bonsai to look like.

Styling your bonsai is one of the most enjoyable parts of keeping these beautiful trees and although there are many styling methods, they are open to the interpretation of the individual. There are guidelines that one can follow to help style their bonsai, but because trees are all unique, they can change according to their normal growth patterns and how you manipulate them.

Once the bonsai has found its definitive seat in the pot, you can devote yourself to the development of the aerial part of the plant.

To do this, bonsai requires continuous attention, ranging from pruning, topping, to the application of metal wire, etc.

All these operations contribute to giving the bonsai a particular shape.

In fact, in bonsai practice, there are many traditional styles that condition the shape of the crown, of the stem, and the branches of the tree according to specific rules.

Starting from the assumption that a bonsai is in all respects a miniature tree and that therefore has its own aesthetic harmony; the styles derive their reason of being from the careful observation and cataloging of the forms of their corresponding "giant cousins."

The bonsai artist tries in a few words to reproduce at bonsai level all those forms that over time nature has produced in normal trees.

Therefore, below we will cover the main styles that regulate the forms of bonsai single or in groups. Before choosing one, however, it is good to look at the plant we have available, looking at it from the height of the pot and not from above, and trying to identify which style best suits its structure.

We are now going to consider all the bonsai styles that are suitable for a single plant.

We will describe: Hokidachi; Chokkan; Moyogi; Shakan; Kengai; Han-Kengai; and that of the twisted trunk.

SINGLE STYLES

Hokidachi style: Hokidachi styling is known as the broom method because the trees are grown remarkably straight with a thick base that gently narrows towards the top. This style is best suited for deciduous trees that have fine branches. The trunk is grown absolutely straight but it doesn't extend all of the way to the top of the tree. Instead, the fine branches grow around the top of the tree and give it a "broomy" look. These branches are pruned to grow around the top third of the tree and this allows leaves, flowers, and even little fruits to decorate the top of the tree.

This style is common amongst beginners because, with the correct support, an enthusiast can guide the trunk of the tree to grow absolutely straight. Other styles require a lot of manipulation where this style requires a straight support next to the stem as it matures. After the tree is matured, the pruning will be simple enough to keep in this style. This is a beautiful and simple style for both beginners and experts.

***Chokkan or erect style*-** The Chokkan style has a completely straight tree, with the strongest and thickest branches growing to a third of its height and thinning more and more going upwards.

The Chokkan style is also very common amongst beginner enthusiasts because it has a straight trunk. It is a style that many trees have in nature, especially if a tree is exposed to a lot of light and doesn't face competition from trees too close together.

The Chokkan is similar to the broom style, but unlike the broom style, this trunk starts thick at the bottom and tapers out as it approaches the top. This is the usual styling of pine trees in nature, and pine bonsais look very similar as they do on a much larger scale. The branches and foliage should be pruned to start growing from as low as a quarter way up from the soil.The branches are arranged symmetrically with respect to the trunk and gradually shorten, giving the tree the image of a cone.

As already mentioned, since the branches must always grow parallel to the ground, it is good to apply the metal wire, if necessary. Conifers are the plants that respond most to this style.

These types of bonsai are particularly beautiful and can be pruned easily. This is one of the best types of bonsai for beginners.

Moyogi or curved trunk style - It is a rather simple style to take care of as it is very natural for the tree. The bonsai has a very balanced shape as the trunk grows straight upwards with some slight curvatures.

The branches grow randomly outside the curvatures and gradually thinner to the top.

The most suitable plants for this style are oaks, beeches and maples.

The Moyogi style is the informal upright style of bonsai that is also readily found in nature. These types of trunks are normally formed in an "S" shape and branches shoot out from each bend. This trunk also starts with a thick base and then tapers out close to the top and grows thick foliage on the top of the tree. This type of bonsai is a prime candidate to accept grafts if the foliage is too thin on the top of the tree.

This type of style can be manipulated but many bonsais, especially ficus and some deciduous trees, will grow naturally into this type of shape if left to their own growth patterns. This style is easy to grow and it's easy to maintain, but it is also beautiful to look at and practically all bonsai enthusiasts are happy with this type of style.

Pruning will tend to give this shape to the tree, especially eliminating the larger branches that grow towards the top of the plant.

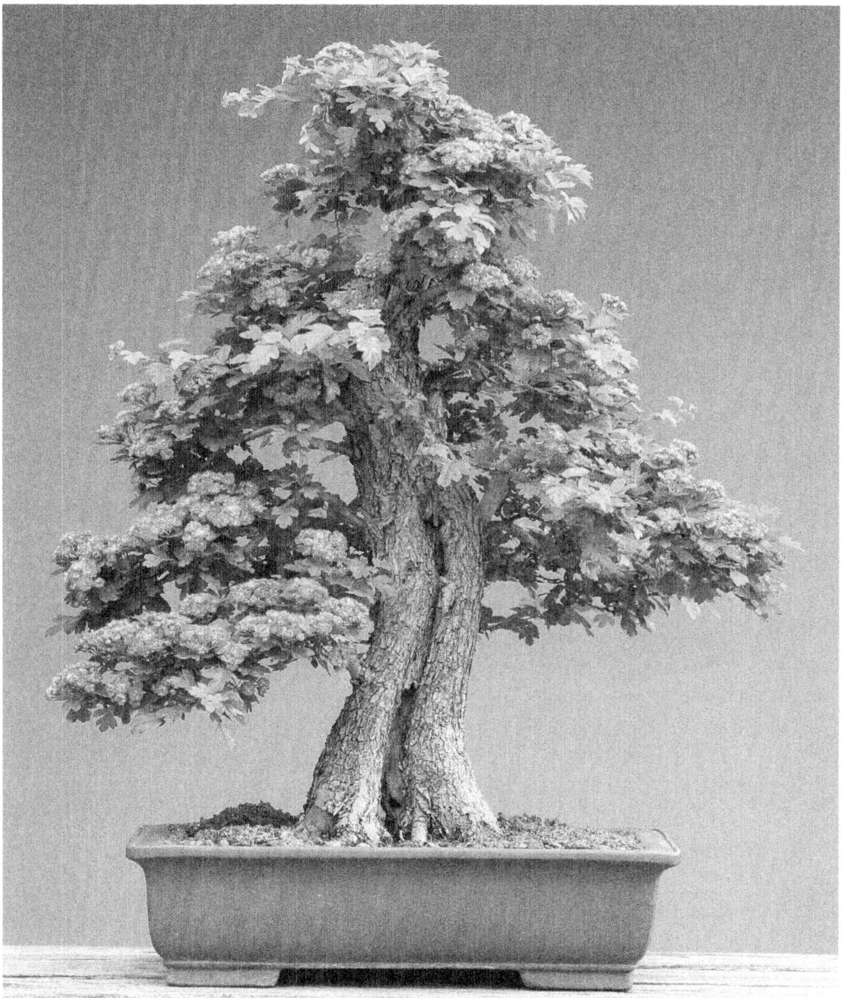

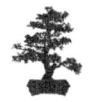

Shakan or sloping trunk style – This style of bonsai is slightly more advanced than the previous three and it occurs in nature when winds blow dominantly in one direction forcing the trees to grow in a particular direction. Trees in valleys and on the sides of mountains are prone to grow like this because wind can be forced down the gradients.

The trunk of the bonsai in this case is no longer upright, but tilted diagonally, forming one or more angles with respect to the ground. The branches grow in all directions and always horizontally.

Characteristic of this style is that the superficial roots protrude from the ground and follow the direction in which the plant inclines.

If an enthusiast wishes to grow their bonsai in this type of style, they would have to ensure that the tree grows at an angle of between 60 and 80 degrees relative to the ground they're planted in. The roots of these types of trees are slightly different from other bonsai, and they will need to be pruned accordingly. The roots on the side opposite to the angle need to be stronger and heavier than the other side of the container, so the weight of the tree can be supported.

When pruning this type of bonsai, it's necessary to ensure that the first branch on the tree is on the opposite side to the tilt, as to work as a form of counter-balance. The image above doesn't have this because the initial trunk is still vertical before the tilt sets in. If the tilt starts from the base, then it's imperative to have a large branch grow off early on to help the tree stay balanced.

This is a more challenging style to grow, but it is a beautiful addition to any enthusiast's collection.

Kengai or waterfall style - This style reproduces the arrangement of those trees that for natural causes have grown in particularly steep places.

The trunk, therefore, bends strongly downwards, coming out of the container, giving the impression of a cascade of leaves. It is important to use a rather tall container, to allow the tree to come out as much as possible, to accentuate the effect more.

Some trees grow on the sides of cliffs but to maintain their balance naturally, some trees grow down and instead of up. The trees germinate and sprout on the cliff and start growing towards the light, but as soon as the tree starts to get heavier, it can't maintain its weight and then starts to grow downward.

Because these trees normally grow on rocks, the availability of nutrients is greatly reduced and the trees don't grow excessively large. After seeing these types of trees in the wild, the Japanese were very interested in growing them for themselves.

This is definitely one of the more difficult styles that you can choose to try and shape your bonsai into because it is unnatural for trees to grow downward. It requires a solid root system and strong but gentle support throughout the entire growth process. This bonsai also requires enough height that it can continue to grow downward, but you have to ensure that it doesn't become too heavy and put excessive weight on the root system.

Kengai, or cascading, bonsai need tall pots and, even though the tree will be grown upright for a while, it will have to be bent into a downward position before the trunk becomes too strong. The flexibility of a young tree (between two and three years) is adequate to safely move into a downward position and continue its growth pattern from there. It may become too risky to move a tree into that type of position after this period because there is a risk of cracking and splintering the trunk. If this happens, the tree will most likely die.

This is an unusual form of bonsai and is one of the more advanced styles, but it is still worth attempting because the results are mesmerizing.

The plants most indicate are conifers and azalea.

Han-Kengai or half-cascade style - This style is very similar to the previous one, except that the trunk comes out of the pot but stays at the edge. Irami are arranged in such a way as to lean slightly downwards, as soon as they come out of the edge, to straighten upwards, immediately afterward. The trees suitable for this style are those of the previous one.

Twisted-trunk style - It is a style that gives a very similar look to the Chokkan one. Also in this case the branches are thinned and shortened towards the top, making the trunk, however, twists on itself, losing to the branches that symmetry that characterizes the Chokkan.

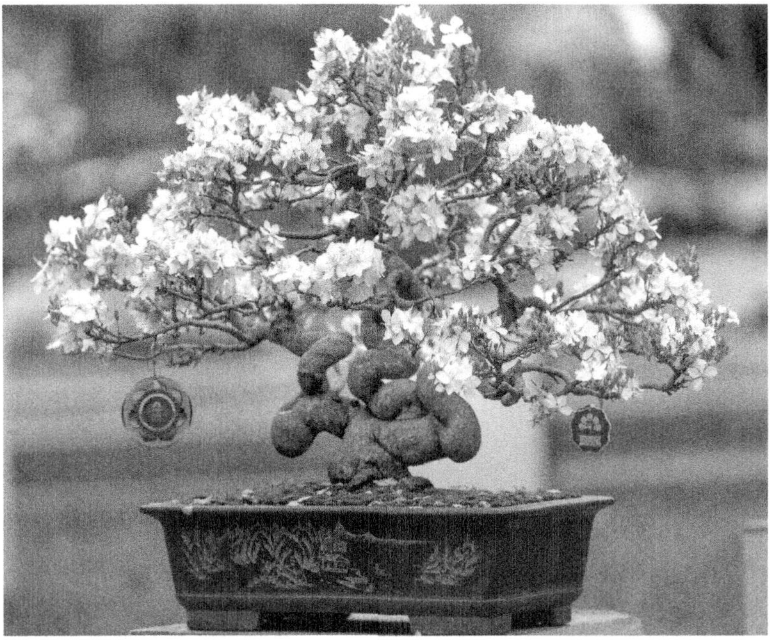

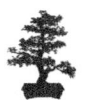

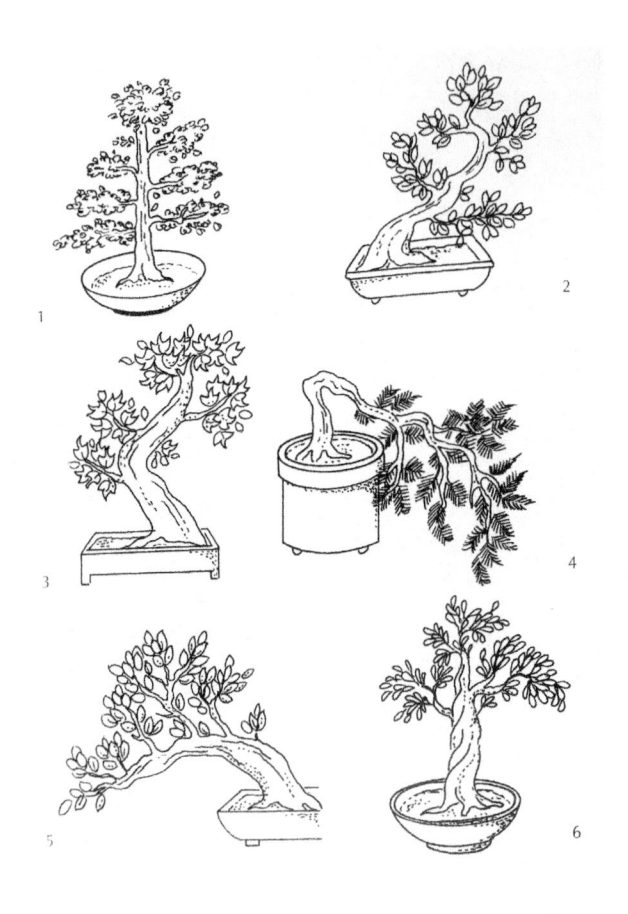

1) Chokkan; 2) Moyogi; 3) Shakan; 4) Kengai;
5) Han-Kengai; 6) Twisted trunk style

GROUP STYLES

Growing bonsai can be rather addictive and as you become more and more confident with certain skills, you might feel like you would like to expand your expertise to a greater level. Having group styles and more than one tree in one container is a great way to start moving into more advanced levels.

Let's now consider those styles that are suitable for groups of bonsai, both those grown from the same root, and those grouped together.

According to Japanese bonsai rules, there should never be a pan number of plants, except for number two.

Sokan or style of the twin trunks- The double and triple-trunk feature (Sokan and Sankan) is common in trees in nature, but it is rather rare to see it as a bonsai.

This style concerns two trees grown from the same root.

It happens for trunks that sprout from the same root system, but because of the confined space, it is rare for bonsai to be able to do this. But when this does happen, the two or three or trunks will vary in length, thickness, and how many branches they produce.

The thicker and most developed trunk will grow upright with one or two other trunks growing outward, but all of the trunks will contribute toward the foliage to make a complete canopy in the years to come.

This isn't necessarily a technique that one can force onto their bonsai and although it can happen naturally, it will require a few extra precautions when repotting these types of bonsais. The roots may intertwine and be very delicate closer to the trunks and damaging them may irreversibly hurt the tree. Thus, take extra care when dealing with these types of bonsai.

The tree that has a more robust trunk is usually called the father, the other son.

The point where the two trees join the root must be as low as possible, so as to give the impression that the bonsai is a composition of two completely autonomous plants.

Sankan or triple trunk style - This style is a variant of the previous one since three twin trees branch off from the root, which must have different sizes to recognize a father, the largest, the son, the minor, and the mother, the one intermediate.

Again, the conjunction with the root should be as low as possible.

Kabudachi or multiple trunk styles – The Kabadachi style is very similar to Sokan and Sankan because it refers to a tree with multiple trunks but they all come from the same root system. Yose-ue, on the other hand, is slightly different because it is the forest form of bonsai collections.

This is arguably one of the most complicated and advanced forms of keeping bonsai because it not only takes patience, it also takes a remarkably gentle hand and significant experience. In these designs, the larger trees are arranged in the middle of the display with the smaller ones on the outskirts to resemble a real forest.

These can be grown from seedlings and nurtured and styled in the same container, or you can move more mature trees into one display. But caution is needed here because the roots of the trees will intertwine and they will be easily damaged. Thus, you will need the help of a few people if you ever had to move the forest bonsai into a larger container so the roots aren't overly damaged.

Always starting as a base from the Sokan, in this style trees are left to grow from the roots in any odd number greater than three, so as to form a small forest.

It is also necessary to remember for this style the importance of the conjunction of plants with roots.

Ikadabuchi or raft style - According to this style, the tree looks like it has fallen to one side and has begun to root downwards and branch upwards, creating new stems that arise from the ground.

For this style, it is better to choose a plant with many branches on one side of the trunk, by cutting or directing the other branches in the right way.

The main trunk must be arranged horizontally and partially covered with earth, making all the branches come out vertically.

As the months go by, new roots will grow in the lower part of the trunk and it will become necessary to cut the original roots of the tree which, until then, were arranged horizontally.

There are also options of growing groups of bonsai on larger pieces of wood, which is known as the raft bonsai style or Ikadabuki. This method is effective because either the wood will start to degrade and give extra nutrients to the bonsai, or the bonsai will find the roots of the wood and start joining their roots with theirs. The conjoining of roots allows for multiple bonsai to grow together with the piece of wood. This method is very successful in group styles because it is less likely for the bonsai to lack nutrients, unlike in rocky terrains, which are far riskier.

Group styles are normally more advanced, but there is no reason for you not to try your hand at some of these styles. Once your confidence has grown in managing single bonsais, you will manage group styles fairly easily.

Netsuranari or sinuous raft style - It is a style that derives from the previous one, from which it differs only for a small feature.

In fact, the trunk of the tree, always arranged horizontally, twists on itself, giving the whole bonsai a sinuous effect.

Yose-ue or forest style -The Yose-ue style refers to the composition of several trees of the same species, but of different ages and sizes, so as to form a miniature forest.

This style requires special preparation and care as, for a good aesthetic result, both spaces and the arrangement of plants must be carefully dosed.

However, it is possible to define some rules that facilitate the composition.

- First of all, it is good to keep in mind already from which angle you want the bonsai to be observed.
  It is therefore recommended to prepare an approximate drawing of the desired arrangement, so as to study the way to prevent two plants from being covered by each other.
- Usually, the trees are arranged in decreasing order of height: In the foreground the larger ones, the medium ones in the center, and at the bottom the smaller ones. This is to give the overall composition a greater three-dimensional effect.
- Always keep in mind that even the empty spaces between the trees have great importance for the harmony of the image.

Great importance also assumes the preparation of the pot in which the bonsai will be planted. This must have a narrow edge and be elongated in shape, large enough to allow each tree adequate root space.

On the bottom of the container, it is necessary to place a wire mesh with tight links, carefully covered with the first layer of gravel and a subsequent layer of bonsai soil.

After arranging the trees, add more soil to the empty spaces and press it carefully.

BOTH SINGLE AND GROUP BONSAI STYLES

We will now see the styles that are suitable for both single and group bonsai.

Hokidachi or inverted broom style- The Hokidachi gives the bonsai an appearance reminiscent of an inverted broom, with the branches starting just above the middle of the stem and fan-shaped upwards until reaching the top. The trunk is erect.

The roots must also be thick and robust and distributed harmoniously in the soil.

A tree suitable for this style, however, is not easy to find in nature, therefore the use of metal wire or even the entire development process from cuttings or by layering is recommended so that the desired shape can be reached more precisely.

Fukinagashi or windswept style - It is a style that requires a lot of care to get good results.

It is rather similar to the Shakan, with the trunk inclined diagonally, with the difference that its branches are not arranged on both sides of the trunk, but extend only on the inclination side, so as to give the impression that the tree is prey to the continuous force of the wind.

It is therefore necessary to cut all the branches that grow on the opposite side to the inclination and let the others thicken and grow stronger.

The branches must always develop horizontally. Even the roots, to respect the image of the tree that fights against the wind, must be very robust and well planted in the ground.

Bunjingi or littered style - This style gives greater importance to the trend of the trunk than to the crown. The bonsai, in fact, is completely bare of branches along the entire length of the stem, except on the top, where small branches develop.

The trunk can be totally erect or have more or less pronounced inclinations, but always so as to maintain a certain harmony of form.

1) Sokan, 2) Sankan, 3) Kabudachi, 4) Ikadabuchi,
5) Netsuranari, 6) Yose-ve

80

ISHITSUKI OR ROCKY STYLE

Ishitsuki is one of the most fascinating styles of bonsai art, as it requires a certain capacity, in addition to offering a remarkable aesthetic effect.

It is called a rock style because inside the container a rock of variable size is placed, which can have two main functions: Either to be simple support for the roots (Ishitsuki on rock) or to be the place where the roots are rooted (Ishitsuki in the rock).

It is good to use rocks that have strong angles and bright colors in order to give a vital image to the composition.

In the event that a rock does not fully satisfy us from the point of view of the shape, it is possible to work with a chisel to bring it closer to our desires.

As for the containers, the oval ones are shallow, with colors and dimensions in harmony with the structure of the rock and the bonsai.

However, the containers usually have neutral colors to counterbalance the more vivid ones of the rock.

Before starting the real work, it is good, also in this case, to make some preliminary sketches to get an idea of how the final composition will look, studying both the point of view from which the bonsai will be observed, both the natural situation and possibly you want to recreate.

It will also be useful to guarantee the bonsai a long and robust root system so that it easily adapts to the new environment in which it will live.

An easy method is to plant the tree in a very deep container and root it well.

Every 3 months 1inch of soil will be removed from the surface of the pot, while keeping the plant at the original height, in order to leave the roots in the open air and to force them to stretch to look for the nourishment in the soil below, The operation will be repeated until the roots have reached a satisfactory length and the plant will then be ready to become a good rocky bonsai.

Now we will examine the differences between the two cases and show how to make a good rocky bonsai.

Ishitsuki on rock – According to this style, the tree is placed on the top of a medium-small rock with the roots that run along with it until it is planted in the ground, giving the impression of wanting to imprison it.

It is, therefore, necessary to choose a tree that has robust roots and arranged in a sunburst pattern and, once placed on the rock, it will contribute to the harmony of the image by cutting the roots too large or too thin.

The tips of the roots are buried in the ground and the others are stopped at the rock to ensure greater stability for the plant.

To do this, it is recommended to use either tape or a metal wire which will be blocked as much as possible inside the cavities of the rock.

After the arrangement, these roots are covered first with a mixture of clay and peat for the thickness of 1 inch, then with the soil wrapped with muslin bandages, it is good to water abundantly and repeatedly, keeping this layer of the soil always moist. In fact, the plant has a great need for nourishment, since the roots are only partially in contact with the earth.

After about 5 months, or in any case, when the roots are sufficiently developed in the pot, muslin and layer of soil on the rock can be eliminated.

From now on the tree is ready to become a good bonsai.

Ishitsuki in the rock- As for Ishitsuki in the rock, the tree is arranged so that the roots penetrate small cavities and root them.

The rock will, therefore, have dimensions large enough to allow this operation.

The most suitable cavity to hold the bonsai is established and it is filled with a light layer of potting soil which will form the basis for the roots.

The bonsai is placed in the cavity, after cleaning the roots and having them covered with soil and peat.

Anchor the tree with wire, as described in Ishitsuki on the rock, making sure that the wire keeps the roots well adhered to the soil of the cables and that the tree is as firm as possible. If necessary, it is good to anchor in several places.

Also, in this case, the soil is constantly kept humid and care will be taken that the bonsai is not exposed too directly to the sun or wind.

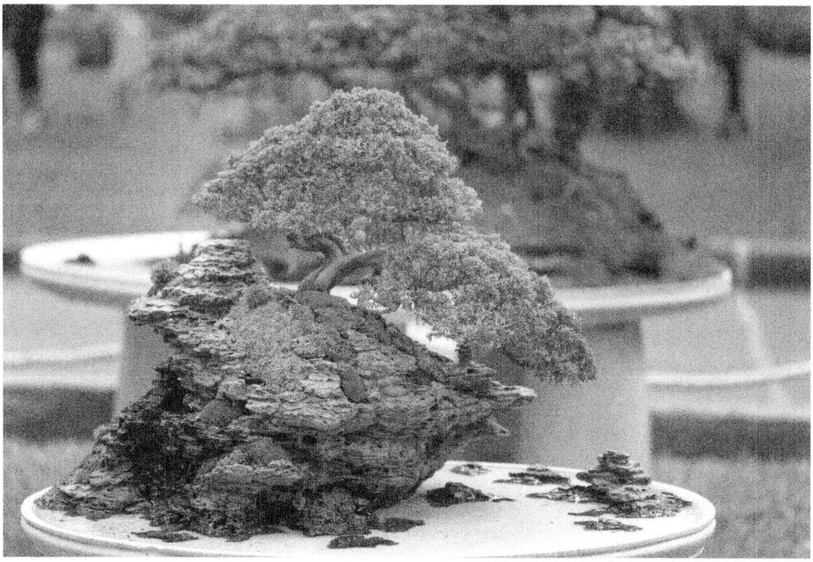

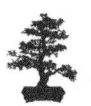

SAIKEI AND BONKEI

These two art forms are related to the nearby bonsai, as they are for creating particular landscapes.

Saikeiin fact is the art of composing a landscape, combining bonsai with small statuettes, houses and buildings of various types.

To compose a similar aspect, you need an idea of a particular and imaginative scenography on which trees and other elements are displayed, giving the impression of observing a portion of nature in miniature.

It is also necessary to carefully take care of the proportions between the various components, as well as the colors and the perspective.

To dare a more natural and wild aspect it is better than the trees are of different ages and sizes, as for every group bonsai.

Bonkei is used in rock saikei. This composition is of particular importance for the Zen tradition, in fact, it implies an attempt to grasp the deep essence of the rock.

All the difficulty, therefore, lies in enhancing the reading of the composition through the arrangement of the elements, the colors, the shapes, up to obtaining a landscape that knows how to show calm and tranquility but also robustness and vital energy

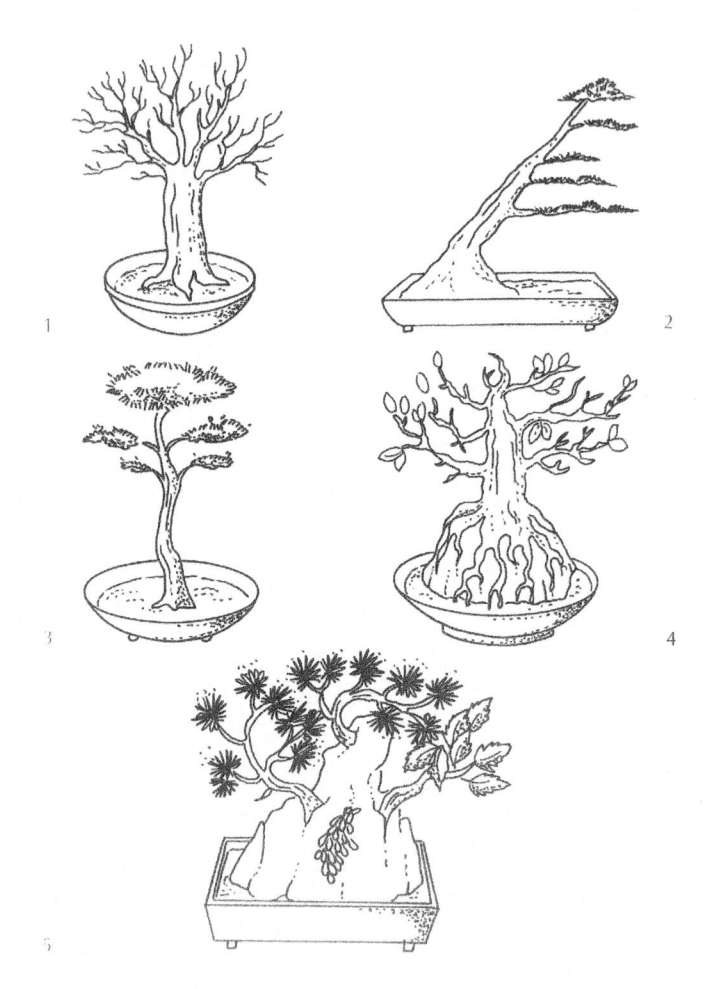

1)Hokidachi; 2) Fukinagashi; 3) Bunjingi; 4)Ishitsuki on the rock; 5) Ishitsuki in the rock

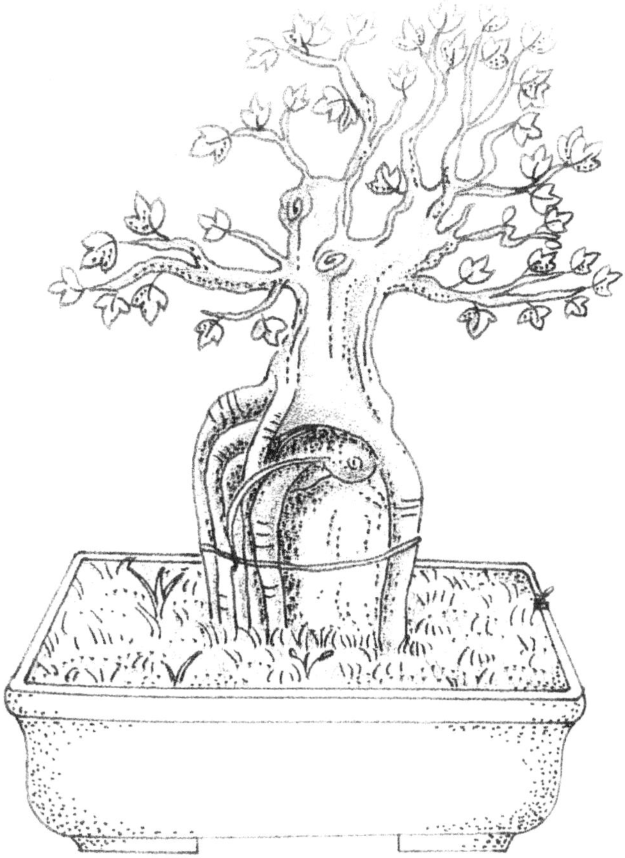

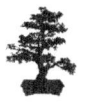

CHAPTER 4 - BONSAI CARE

We are now going to take a closer look at the actual work that characterizes bonsai art, starting from the fundamental part that concerns pruning up to the simplest, but no less important, operations of watering and fertilization.

First of all, it is good to know that bonsai needs daily care and needs, like all plants, to maintain particular rhythms and habits.

The ability of a bonsai artist also lies in being able to respect the woods of his plant. However, there are some rules that it is good to follow to get a good bonsai, and that concern each of the five parts of which a plant is made, starting from the roots to get to the top.

Let's see them in detail:

- **Roots:** It is important that the roots develop in all directions so as to allow a better grip on the ground and more adequate nourishment.
- **Trunk:** The trunks must have a solid and robust base and progressively thin upwards. The older the trunk appears, worn from years and from natural damage, such as cracks in the bark, lightning strikes, the more the bonsai acquires value.
- **Branches:** The branches must have a fixed arrangement, the larger ones must extend to the sides, while the smaller ones upwards. The branches that grow on the front, those that start from the same point of the trunk, and those that develop horizontally in a regular way are not very appreciated.

- **Leaves:** The leaves must always be proportionate to the rest of the bonsai. They must remain small and cover the branches creating a thick crown.
- **Top:** The top in the bonsai tradition symbolizes life, it must, therefore, be vital and robust. A broken or ruined top is never considered valuable, except when it gives the tree a desired air of austerity.

PRUNING

One of the most important ways to make your bonsai grow in the way that you want it to is to prune it on a semi-regular basis.

Pruning, in fact, is the main job that allows us to keep a small tree, as it gives us the opportunity to modify and control the natural plant development.

By cutting a branch, in fact, it is prevented from continuing to grow and forces them to develop small sub-branches that will form a 10 crown.

However, it is good to consider that there are different ways of pruning depending on the style and the type of tree you want to grow.

There are two different types of pruning techniques that are needed: maintenance pruning, which refines and maintains the structure of the bonsai; and structural pruning, which is more aggressive but gives the bonsai a more basic or natural style.

Before knowing the difference between these two techniques, it is important to fully understand how trees grow and act within their natural environment. Understanding how trees grow and why they respond to certain conditions will help you prune them effectively.

Trees, naturally, have a tendency toward apical dominance, which means their trunks will almost always grow bigger and stronger than their side stems and other offshoots. And this dominance carries on throughout the entire tree. The main trunk has smaller branches, but those smaller branches will be dominant over other smaller branches. This sequence carries on until only the foliage is left.

This is a natural mechanism that many trees have to grow taller instead of casting shade over other trees next to them. But this apical dominance also causes the tree to keep distributing growth to the top and outer branches and this ultimately causes the inner branches to die. This is normal in nature, but it can be aesthetically unpleasing to the eye in the world of growing bonsais.

Once an enthusiast knows the natural growth patterns of a tree, they are able to use pruning techniques to counter the negative aesthetic effects of apical dominance. Since dominant growth occurs in a tree's trunk, it's easy to surmise that the top and outer portions of the bonsai should be pruned more thoroughly. This pruning forces the tree to redistribute growth to the inner and lower parts of the tree, which gives the enthusiast control over the growth of the tree, the thickness of the trunk, and the overall aesthetics of the bonsai.

STRUCTURAL PRUNING

If you have grown your bonsai from a seed/seedling and you have waited for a few years for it to get to the place where you can start pruning it, there will come a time where the tree is strong enough to be pruned and shaped according to what you would like. Structural pruning involves removing larger branches from your bonsai and shaping it into the tree that you want it to be. But, this is a rather stressful process for most enthusiasts because even though the large branches will grow back, the first structural pruning will determine the growth pattern and the overall look of the bonsai. Therefore, it's necessary to carefully consider what type of style you would like for your bonsai. Do take into consideration what species of tree you are growing and what styles suit it.

Once you have considered the style and decided on the right one, carefully consider which branches would need to be pruned to start the process of the style.

Because these prunings are rather traumatic on the bonsai, it's better to rather perform them in early spring or late autumn. This enables the bonsai to either enter or exit a growing season. Both of these are normally successful, but if your species of bonsai doesn't cope well in cold weather, it will be better not to prune it in late autumn because the tree will have the combination of cold weather and the trauma of pruning which may kill it.

To start this type of pruning, place your bonsai on a table and look at it from eye level. Start by removing all of the dead foliage and branches from the tree. Once that is completed, start analyzing the bonsai and decide which larger branches you want to remove. This includes all of the branches that block the view of the main trunk, branches that cross over with each other, and disproportionately thick branches at the top of the bonsai.

It is an unfortunate fact that pruning thick branches will leave scarring on the bonsai but this can be reduced if you use concave bonsai cutters. Since your bonsai is an aesthetic work of art, it is worth investing in these types of cutters to reduce the effects of scarring and keep the bonsai as pristine as possible.

If your bonsai is healthy, you can safely remove up to ⅓ of its foliage (which is the same percentage of roots you are allowed to prune before putting your bonsai in danger), but this type of "big" maintenance should only be performed once a year. Anything more can, and most likely will, damage your tree and cause it to die prematurely.

Before embarking on the pruning operation, you must have a clear understanding of the shape you want to give the plant so that you know where to start.

We take the appropriate tools, such as simple bonsai and bud shears, and get to work, remembering some basic rules, which are indispensable for obtaining the necessary effects of harmony and balance.

First of all, the branches must not grow in the lower part of the trunk.

Usually, the branches are started to develop at a third of the total length of the trunk, to give the plant greater impetus.

It is important to take into great consideration the point where the plant is observed; in this way, it will be evident, as we have seen, that the branches that grow on the front of the plant are useless, while those on the sides and on the back will be accentuated.

To give a livelier image to the bonsai, while maintaining a harmonious appearance, it is good to avoid the branches that grow at the same height and parallel, and also, during pruning, remember not to prune all the branches to the same size, but to leave different lengths.

If you want to limit the growth of a branch, to keep it small, it is sufficient to trim it, otherwise, it will develop and strengthen.

It is advisable to carry out pruning in the period of the year in which the crown is developed, so as to have undergone a clear image of the cuts that are being practiced on the bonsai.

Finally, it is very important, when you want to cut a whole branch, as close as possible to the trunk, by leveling the cut, so as to hide the wound from sight.

For this purpose, the use of concave shears is recommended.

In addition, in the case of particularly deep wounds, it is good to use a suitable disinfectant to be purchased from a nurseryman.

Sometimes to give an older image to the bonsai, a special tool is used, called a jinning forceps.

This allows the branches to be cut so as to leave part of the bark of the branch attached to the trunk, giving the impression that the tree has been affected by lightning.

For use of pruning to direct the growth of branches. By pruning the branch, a just above a bud facing downwards we will obtain a branch that will grow upwards after drawing a curve.

The dashes in the two sequences, show the branches that are of no use for the formation of any bonsai style, therefore they must be pruned

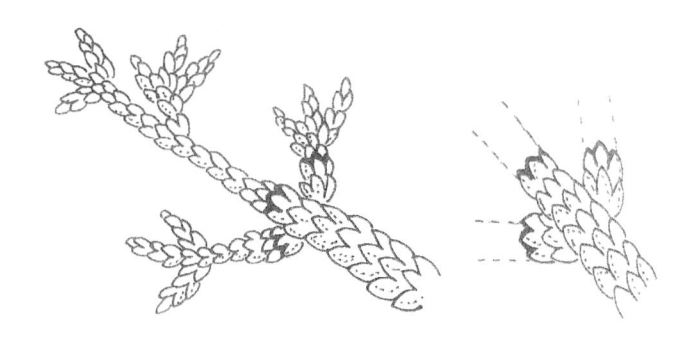

How to trim the shoots of a conifer

This technique is particularly difficult and still requires some experience in order not to ruin the plant.

Finally, it's advisable to do some shopping online and purchase a cut-paste that you can apply to all of the wounds on the bonsai after pruning. Infections in trees aren't uncommon and if you have spent a lot of time and effort on your bonsai, the last thing you want to do is lose it because of a bad cut. Bonsai cut-pastes prevent infections and promote faster healing.

MAINTENANCE PRUNING

The primary goal of maintenance pruning is to prevent a bonsai from acting as it would in nature. Once a tree starts to focus its growth towards the top and outer branches, the bonsai doesn't really look pleasing to the eye any longer. So, maintenance pruning needs to be employed on a regular basis to keep it from growing in areas where it isn't supposed to. When those areas are pruned away, the tree naturally sends the nutrients to the trunk and starts to increase in size centrally — this results in a much better-looking bonsai.

If you are unsure when to prune your bonsai, it depends on whether you keep your bonsai outdoors or indoors. Outdoor bonsais should only be pruned during the growing seasons of spring and summer. Since the cold makes the tree go dormant and doesn't send a lot of nutrients to the foliage, it's redundant to prune during the cold months. But, if you have an indoor bonsai, you can prune all-year-round because the bonsai will remain warmer inside and, thus, not have a dormant period.

Unlike pruning rose bushes, you don't need to excessively prune your bonsai when you're maintaining its shape. Only prune the areas that start growing too quickly. If a branch becomes too long or the canopy is uneven, then snip those parts off.

Use sharp scissors to snip away at the branches and maintain the leaves, but if you have a pine or another coniferous bonsai, it's better to rather pinch the branches off with your fingers because snipping it with scissors can lead to unsightly brown discolorations and dead foliage at the pruning sites. Since the bonsai is still small, the branches are tender enough to easily be pinched off by hand.

Some bonsais are better pruned with scissors, while others are better pruned with your fingers, but some actually need a combination of the two depending on the type of tree and strength of the branches. Hence, adequate research on your bonsai is necessary to know exactly what is the best method of maintenance pruning.

CUTTING LEAVES AND BUDS

It happens that an indoor bonsai throws the buds all year round, so pruning leaves and buds are an almost daily practice.

However, it is easy to apply, in fact, the rules to follow are less numerous than for pruning branches.

The important thing is to remember that where a sprout is left there, a branch will develop, while the lower part of the trunk will be strengthened and the branching will become thinner.

In any case, it is good to remember that the leaves must always be cut leaving a piece of a stalk and that the direction of the last leaf a stalk left after cutting also determines the direction of the bud that will grow later.

It is recommended to always cut the biggest leaves. As for the plants that bloom, pruning will only be done after the development of the flowers.

While for subtropical plants the right period for cutting shoots and leaves is between spring and autumn, tropical plants, which grow all year round, will always be pruned and pruned.

In conifers, the topping of the shoots, an operation sometimes performed simply with the nails, will cause many small needles to develop. In short, the cutting of the leaves allows us to obtain three main results: A thin branching, the shrinking of the leaves and greater ventilation of the crown of the branches.

Every year, in the period between March and August, it is good to proceed with the total defoliation of the tree; in doing so, the plant is stimulated to develop new shoots in a short time, accelerating vegetative growth.

Smaller leaves and thinner branches will grow under the petioles, giving the bonsai the classic appearance of a dwarf tree.

Effects of leaf pruning

APPLICATION OF THE METAL WIRE

We now pass to another very important moment, that of the application of the metal wire, which is essential for the tree to grow according to the desired shape.

Pruning is a very important part of shaping your bonsai, but if you want to truly shape your bonsai into the shape you desire, then you will need to take it a step further and wire your bonsai.

By wrapping wire around the trunk and branches of your bonsai, you are able to manipulate exactly where and how you want the branches to grow. When the tree is flexible, it's easy to move the bonsai into the position that you would like, but it's rather complicated to keep it there. Having the sturdiness of the wire allows for the tree to be molded and then remain in the position it was placed in. It will take a few months, but as soon as the branches are set, the wire can be removed. The bonsai will continue to grow in the style that it was adjusted into.

Bonsais can be wired at any time of year and it can be performed at your own preference. The only species of trees that should be wired in winter are deciduous trees and any other trees that lose their leaves in colder temperatures. The reason for this is because it's much easier to wire the bonsais when your vision isn't obstructed by foliage. But it is important to pay attention during this time because even though the nutrients in foliage don't go to the foliage, large branches can grow thicker in the winter months and, if this occurs, it can create scarring if the wires start digging into the flesh of the branches.

If you notice that the branches are growing at an accelerated rate, remove the wiring around the bonsai and replace it at a later stage. Scarring from wires that have broken the bark of a bonsai will most likely be permanent, so it should be avoided as best as possible.

TYPES OF WIRES

There are two types of wires that can be considered when wiring bonsais:

Suitable wires are copper or aluminum and for some types of trees, such as maple, apricot and thorns, it is convenient to use plastic-coated threads or wrapped in paper.

Neither one of these wires rust and both have a strong tensile strength. Aluminum wire is better for use in deciduous bonsais, while copper wire is better for use in pine and conifer trees. That being said, the aluminum wire does work well with practically all species of bonsais and is the easiest to use as a beginner enthusiast.

The diameter will be of different sizes depending on the thickness and strength of the branch to be corrected.

Usually, a wire 1/3 of the diameter of the branch or trunk to be wrapped is used.

Wires come in a variety of thicknesses (1 - 8 mm) but the best ones for beginners don't exceed 4 mm in thickness. The thicker wires should be used on the larger branches and you can use thinner wires as you move up and along the bonsai. It is best to first wrap the trunk and thick branches in palm fiber (raffia) that has been soaked in water. This prevents scarring on the thicker sections of the bonsai. If thinner branches are scarred, they can always be removed, but this isn't a possibility with the trunk and main branches. So extra precautions are necessary.

HOW TO WIRE YOUR BONSAI

Wiring your bonsai is going to be very tricky and you are going to make mistakes. But as you have learned to be more patient with the entire growing process of your bonsai, you will get the technique right when you practice it. While you are still starting out, consider double-wiring certain branches that are close together because wrapping them together allows support for the branches and allows slightly more space for you to work.

Before proceeding with the application, it is advisable to fix the wire to the ground or to the trunk, always starting from the backside, so as to hide the origin of the binding or not to leave too much play.

Especially for the first case, in fact, it would damage the bark of the tree, risking the wire embedding itself in the bonsai. In this case, it is better to cut the metal wire and leave the part embedded in the shaft, to avoid even greater injuries.

The wire should be wound at an angle of 45 degrees to the trunk or branch, avoiding tying both leaves and buds.

The period of time in which to maintain the binding is different depending on the style chosen and the type of tree: Indicatively, it varies from 6-8 months of deciduous plants to 18 months of conifers.

The thread will preferably be removed in the autumn before the vegetative stasis. It is good to remember not to apply during the vegetative awakening of the plant, not to practice it on newly repotted or repotted bonsai trees, as each of these operations considerably weakens the plant.

Once the wire has been applied, the plant will be kept in a place sheltered from the sun and wind, spraying and watering often.

The metal wire is the main technique for changing the shape of the plant; however, there are other ways to correct it.

Once you have got the hang of this method, use single-wiring on the branches that can't be double-wired. Don't shape the branches until you have wrapped the entire tree because if you start shaping it too early you may get confused with what to do with the remainder of the branches if you designed your desired style. Waiting until the end to shape allows you to move everything more smoothly and sequentially.

When wiring an entire bonsai, start at the bottom of the trunk and then move up to the primary branches. Once those are done, use a thinner wire to wrap the secondary branches and up into the foliage. As a general rule, use a wire that is ⅓ as thick as the branch that you are wiring. That thickness will allow for enough structural support to style the bonsai.

After you have completed the entire process of wiring the bonsai (which will take a long time, so be patient), you can start to form it into the shape you desire. Grip the branches firmly with your thumb and index finger and start bending them slowly. Even though the branches are flexible, they can still break, so move slowly and gently. Once the branch is positioned, do not move it again.

Once your bonsai has been styled according to your specifications, move it outside and into a shady spot if it's in the warmer months. Fertilize your bonsai as you normally would and keep a close eye on it because you don't want the tree to grow and get scarred. When you remove the wiring, you need to cut the wires at every turn and not unwind it. Unwinding the wiring almost always damages the bark on the bonsai and it will leave avoidable scarring.

In fact, you can also use cords attached to the container, to another support, or to the trunk itself to keep the branches in tension.

Other times stones or weights can be tied to a branch in order to change its direction of development.

Finally, with small wooden dowels, it is possible to spread two branches considered too close.

Of all these techniques, however, that of the metal wire is the most used, as it allows a more precise action on the branches and on the trunk.

WATERING AND FERTILIZING

There are several fundamentals of growing bonsais but two of the most integral are watering and fertilizing sufficiently. These factors are all dependent on the species of the bonsai, the size of the tree, the season, the size of the container, and how much sunlight the bonsai receives. It is necessary to research exactly how much water and fertilizer your bonsai needs, but there are a few basic guidelines that you can follow to ensure that your bonsai remains healthy.

SUCCESSFUL WATERING

The first rule of successful watering is not to water your tree while the soil is still wet, but it's also important not to let the soil get dry either. There needs to be a careful balance between the two because overly wet soil can cause root rot and too dry soil can cause the roots to become brittle which will cause them to die. While you are still learning how to judge this process, place your finger about ½ an inch into the soil and feel for the moisture content. If you think that it's becoming slightly dry, then you should water your tree. The longer you perform this, the more experience you will gain and the more you will be able to judge by sight when your bonsai needs to be watered.

The second rule is never to water on a routine. If you have multiple bonsai, you may be tempted to water on a routine, but this can be detrimental to your trees because you may be overwatering some and underwatering others. Judge each bonsai individually and ensure that they all receive water when they need it.

The final rule is to water gently. Water that's being poured out rapidly can move the soil too rapidly and damage some of the roots. It's imperative to use a watering can that has a fine nozzle to disperse the water evenly over the top of the soil without displacing it. This type of nozzle will also keep you from overwatering your bonsais.

Watering, so it is another very important phase in the care of a bonsai. It must be practiced often with extreme care, so as not to damage the plant. The bonsai, in fact, because of its restricted root system, it does not draw sustenance from the soil for a long time.

It is therefore necessary to keep it supplied with moist soil rich in nutrients. It is a good rule to water the soil only when it is dry or slightly damp; watering when the soil is still wet can cause more damage than advantages.

Some tricks allow us, however, to easily understand if it is really necessary to water. The first concerns the color that the soil takes on: it will be drier the more the color becomes clear.

A dark color instead indicates that the earth is still steeped in water.

The need for water from the bonsai can also be ascertained by simply knocking against the container and listening to the sound produced.

Usually, an empty sound shows that the earth has dried up, detaching itself from the edges of the vase; on the contrary, a full muffled sound will indicate that the earth is dilated by water and adheres well to the container.

Two methods are mainly used for watering: Either the water is poured onto the soil surface through a watering can, or the container is directly immersed in the water. In the first case, it will be necessary to proceed slowly, to allow time for the soil to fully impregnate.

When the water comes out of the drain hole, the soil will have been properly watered. In the event, however, that the water cannot penetrate the soil, but escapes from the edge of the container, it means that the earth is too dry and we will proceed in the other way.

The second method is equally simple. The containers are immersed in water to bring bubbles of air to the surface. When no more bubbles come out, the soil will be completely drenched with water and the bonsai can be rearranged in its place.

The bonsai however change their water needs in the changing seasons. In summer it will be necessary to water more frequently, at least twice a day, making sure that the soil does not dry out too much. However, we recommend watering early in the morning and in the evening with water at room temperature.

Furthermore, especially in the city, it is important to spray the leaves during the day to eliminate the smog and dust layer that can be created. However, you have to remember not to do it in the evening, because the plant could get sick or be damaged in any case.

Furthermore, during the summer period, miniature and rock bonsai trees need more water than normal bonsai, as well as deciduous trees since the rather large surface of the leaves increases transudation.

In the autumn season, however, the need for water decreases, the leaves fall, and the plant prepares for winter stasis. In any case, it will be good to frequently check the humidity conditions in order not to experience unpleasant inconveniences.

With winter, the phase of least demand for water is reached, as the tree slows down most of its functions and enters a period of substantial inactivity.

It is therefore sufficient to water 2-3 times a week, preferably during the afternoon hours to avoid night frost.

Only conifers maintain their need for water rather high since the foliar apparatus does not fall during the autumn and needs continuous nourishment.

With spring, however, the full activity of the tree begins again, the shoots reappear and the demand for water resumes, which will increase more and more over time, as we get closer to summer.

SUCCESSFUL FERTILIZING

Any gardener knows that fertilizing their plants from time to time will ensure their health and make them far more vibrant, and this is a mentality that all bonsai enthusiasts need to adopt too. Because fertilizing your bonsai regularly during the growing season is paramount for the tree to not only survive but to thrive.

As with all plants, bonsais require a fertilizer that's well-balanced in nitrogen, potassium, and phosphorus. There are times that you can change the concentrations, but that is normally reserved for expert-level enthusiasts. As a beginner enthusiast, it is encouraged just to use fertilizers that are equal in all three amounts with other micronutrients included.

During the growth period, fertilization must be carried out every twenty days, going as far as fertilizing also every week, during the autumn, to prepare the plant for the winter period. In winter, fertilization is superfluous for many bonsai as the plant stops its vegetative development.

Only conifers are to be fertilized as early as January as they resume activity before other plants. Fertilization should always be carried out after the flowering period, to prevent the flowering branches from absorbing too much nourishment and losing the flowers. Remember also that it is good not to start immediately after repotting or pruning the roots, as the injured parts would be damaged.

It's necessary to follow the specifications on the fertilizer you purchase. Some fertilizers are more concentrated than others and overfeeding your bonsai is a possibility. But bonsai fertilizers normally come in cubes and can be included directly on the ground around the bonsai itself. However, these fertilizer cubes can be picked up by birds if you have your bonsai outside so you will need to protect them. It's best to cover them with cups or baskets that allow water to pass through easily. Water as you normally would until the fertilizer cubes are dissolved.

Alternatively, bonsai fertilizer can also be purchased in liquid form. This can be diluted directly into your watering can and gradually given to your bonsais. Both of these fertilizers are effective and you can use whichever you prefer.

Remember that because the amount of soil in a bonsai pot is limited, there is a limited amount of nutrients available for the tree to use. This means that your bonsai will need extra nutrients from fertilizers. But keep in mind that overfeeding your tree can kill it too, so carefully balance the feeding regime with the guidelines on the fertilizer you purchase.

Fertilizers, furthermore if used correctly, are indispensable to help the development of our bonsai, by integrating and completing the nutrients of the soil.

Deprived of fertilizers the bonsai would live for about a year, therefore it would begin to perish, the leaves would wither and branches and trunk would weaken.

This is because the bonsai, being forced into a pot of such a small size after a certain period exhausts the mineral elements necessary for its nourishment.

It is therefore important to remember that every bonsai needs a certain amount of nitrogen, phosphorus, potassium, calcium, sulfur, iron and, in smaller quantities, other minerals.

We will, therefore, have to look for fertilizers that contain these substances.

Various types of fertilizers are available on the market: Powder, liquids and balls, the latter used mainly for outdoor bonsai but also very suitable for indoor bonsai.

Furthermore, a distinction is also made between organic fertilizers, namely those derived from organic fabrics, such as bone meal, blood-based fertilizers, etc., and inorganic fertilizers, such as salt compounds.

For good fertilization, it is however essential to follow some rules.

First of all, the fertilizer should be administered especially during the growing season of the plant, helping it with all the necessary nourishment; it is, the youngest bonsai to need more help, precisely for their very rapid growth.

Once you have chosen the most suitable period and the type of fertilizer you can move on to the practical phase.

Water abundantly and prepare the dose of fertilizer as indicated on the package; in fact, the dose for a bonsai does not differ much from that normally recommended.

This is how we proceed to fertilization, remembering these tips:
- It is always better to fertilize little, but often, rather than a lot and rarely because in this way the food is distributed more regularly over time, without risking excesses.
- Liquid fertilizers are absorbed faster, so it will be necessary to fertilize more often. On the contrary, powder fertilizers dissolve more slowly in the soil, allowing a lasting effect.

If the roots get sick, it is good to stop fertilizing until the root system is completely restored

CHAPTER 5 - PLANT DISEASES

We now begin a very important chapter in the care of bonsai, as it can often happen that a plant shows symptoms of a disease that is difficult to recognize and, therefore, to cure. In fact, due to its size, the bonsai is more defenseless than the normal plants against the attacks of many adversities, therefore it is the bonsai artist's job to quickly recognize the diseases and help his plant.

When the bonsai begins to weaken, it is immediately necessary to check whether there are deficiencies or excesses of some kind in its care and maintenance: In what position is the plant about to the wind and light? At what level are humidity and temperature? Is it fed in the right way? All these factors must always be kept under control, but sometimes the bad health of our bonsai can derive from other causes.

Bonsai trees, like most other plants on earth, are susceptible to parasites, fungi, and insects that can greatly damage them. Since there are so many things that can attack your bonsai, the best case of treatment, in this case, is prevention. If you keep your tree healthy, it will be able to fight off many infections and fungi without much external help, because many trees can mount their own defenses against these attacks.

If you balance your water, fertilizer, and light requirements for your bonsai, it will most likely stay healthy and continue to grow for years. But one of the worst problems that enthusiasts make is to put their bonsai in the wrong location. If the tree doesn't have good lighting and good air circulation, it will be more susceptible to developing a problem.

Additionally, it is necessary that you keep the area around your bonsai as hygienic as possible. If you take the effort of cleaning the area where your bonsais are situated, there is a greatly reduced risk of your tree(s) developing problems, but sometimes there are problems that can arise that even healthy trees can't ward off — pests.

ANIMAL AND PLANT PESTS

It is important to bear in mind that bonsai are subject to the same pests and diseases as the species of the trees to which they belong. Therefore, in principle, as regards diseases due to plant or animal parasites, a bonsai, if in full force, has the potential to defend itself.

A constant cure would, therefore, be sufficient to prevent and avoid diseases of this type.

However, this does not exclude that, during the weakening phases due to repotting or pruning, the bonsai can get sick.

Among the animal parasites, we find various types of insects that damage the plant by using it for their nourishment.

The most common are:

- **Ants**

Description: Ants on your bonsai are a dangerous sign because ants and aphids normally work together. The reason for this is because ants and aphids have a co-dependent relationship where the ants carry the eggs of aphids to suitable vegetation because the aphids will eventually produce a sweet, sugary substance known as "honeydew" which the ants thrive on. The ants aren't really a problem on your bonsai, but their little passengers are definitely something to worry about.

Ants may not be a problem themselves, but the problems that they carry with them can be severely devastating to your bonsai. Ants don't only carry aphid eggs, but they can also carry a black sooty fungus that starts to destroy the bark of trees. Additionally, ants are known to make their nests in bonsai pots and can disrupt the root system of your bonsai.

Symptoms:If you notice that ants are starting to nest in your bonsai's pot, then it indicates that you aren't watering your tree correctly. But, in the cases of trees like pines, which prefer drier soil, sometimes this can't be changed because adding additional water could hurt your tree.

Cure: In cases like these, it's better to use a gentle pesticide that won't hurt the roots of your tree. Pesticides like Bungy, Kemprin, and Koinor are your best options for treating problems at a root level.

- *Anthracnose*

Description: Anthracnose is an umbrella term that includes several fungal infections that affect trees. These fungi thrive on plant material where it inoculates and then spreads very quickly. If a bonsai is kept in a warm, humid, shady place, these fungi will spread like wildfire and damage your bonsai.

Unfortunately, during the warmth of the growing seasons along with young foliage starting to develop, anthracnose is a serious risk and you need to keep a close eye on any signs of it developing. When leaves become thicker and more leathery, they are far more resilient to fungal infections, but young leaves are very susceptible.

Symptoms: The symptoms of these types of infections are very easy to spot, but they still seem to go unnoticed by enthusiasts who don't know what they're looking for. One of the indicative symptoms is the drying and curling of leaves that look like they've been burned. As the fungal infection worsens, more and more brown spots will spread to more leaves and will continuously look like the tree is being scorched even though it may be in a shady spot.

Not all trees are susceptible to these types of infections and they are practically unheard of in species like conifers and evergreens. Deciduous trees, on the other hand, have much softer leaves and seem to be far more susceptible to these types of infections

Even though these types of infections are rather unsightly on your bonsai, they aren't normally severe enough to kill the tree. They usually only cause the death of one or two branches at a time, but if left untreated, it can eventually spread into the trunk of the tree and that can lead to its death.

Cure: If you notice that your bonsai is infected with this type of infection, it will spread to your other trees and plants if you aren't careful. It is important to quarantine any bonsais with these possible infections and keep them away from other plants. Just like human infections, these types of infections can spread very easily to any other plants close to them so quarantining them is one of the best actions.

Once that is done, spray your tree with chemical sprays designed to treat anthracnose infections and repeat the treatment until it starts working. It is also necessary to remove all of the infected leaves and branches as far as possible and spray the rest of the tree down on a daily basis. Keep the tree in a highly lit area and watch the bonsai closely for any brown spots on the uninfected leaves.

- *Aphids*

Description: Even though an infestation of ants is normally indicative of an aphid infestation, aphids are also known to attack plants by themselves. Aphids are one of the most common and one of the most detrimental pests to bonsais. Aphids burrow into the soft areas of plants and start sucking out the sap. But this has a dual problem because the plant is losing a lot of its nutrients and aphids regularly carry diseases that attack plants from the inside.

Any little bugs that appear to be green, black, or gray are most likely aphids and if you spot them, they should be treated quickly. Aphids attack plants and manage to devour large sections of the plants in a very small amount of time, so it's important to check under your bonsai's leaves on a regular basis to keep any problems from arising.

Symptoms: If you notice that the leaves and branches on your bonsai seem to be weaker than normal, it could be indicative of an aphid attack. Additionally, if you notice that new leaves that are sprouting seem to be curled and unhealthy, then your suspicions may be confirmed. The reason why the new growth comes out looking like that is that the nutrients are so leached out by the aphids that the tree can't adequately support new growth.

Cure: If this is a problem that is affecting your bonsai, then you will need to wash the leaves with a stream of water. But ensure that you don't harm the tree further. Additionally, there are some gentle baby shampoos that can be used. Make a diluted solution and wash the leaves. The aphids can't breathe with the soap covering them and they either leave or die. A few repetitions of this should clear up the infestation.

You can consider other insecticides or you can move your bonsai to an area that has a high population of ladybugs. Ladybugs are carnivorous little beetles and they devour aphids without harming your bonsai. There are many insects that you want in your garden and ladybugs are definitely one of them!

- **Borer**

Description: Tree borers consist of different species of insects that lay their eggs on or underneath a tree's bark. When the eggs hatch and the larvae start to squirm out, they immediately look for sustenance and they start to burrow deeper into the tree, eating the woody flesh as they move deeper.

As the larvae grow, their appetites will also increase, and because they may be burrowing into the trunk of your bonsai, there may be serious problems that will develop soon after they get deeper into the lumen.

Symptoms: It is possible to miss the adult insects on your bonsai, but you will notice the signs that larvae have started to burrow into your bonsai. There will be signs of holes and even sawdust around the base of the tree.

Cure: This type of infestation is definitely one of the most difficult to treat and if the larvae have made it into the trunk, it might be untreatable. There are pesticides that you can try, but the real problem is that the death of the wood is going to affect your bonsai's aesthetics forever. If you have other bonsai, it might be best to get rid of the infected bonsai to prevent it from spreading to any of your other trees.

It may be a difficult decision, but it may be the most prudent in cases like these.

- *Caterpillars*

Description: Caterpillars are the larvae stage of butterflies and moths and even though most of their damage is caused above ground, they do have voracious appetites.

Symptoms: Caterpillars of all sixes can consume large quantities of leaves in a very small space of time.

Fortunately, it's very easy to see if caterpillars have attacked your bonsai and you will be able to take action quickly.

Cure: The best treatment, in this case, is to actually remove them by hand. This may be time-consuming, and some caterpillars are small and camouflaged, but it is better for your bonsai and the environment if you are able to avoid using pesticides. It is also useful to make a solution of baby shampoo and rub it on the leaves of your bonsai. If there is a form of soap on the leaves, the caterpillars won't want to eat them.

- **Mealybugs**

Description: Mealybugs are white, furry insects that produce a waxy covering to protect themselves from the elements and from larger predators. These types of insects are found underneath leaves and sometimes in the root systems of plants. So, when you are repotting your bonsai, it's always necessary to check the roots for any indications of these little creatures.

Symptoms: Just like aphids, mealybugs burrow in and start sucking the sap of the tree or plant. Leaves will start to droop and look unhealthy. They will move from vibrant green to a more yellow discoloration until the leaf dies. If left untreated, the tree will take strain because of the lack of nutrients so it does need to be addressed quickly.

Cure: Using an acidic solution of lime or lemon juice in these cases helps for the treatment of mealy bugs and the acid can effectively kill them. If this isn't successful you can increase the treatment to a pesticide that is safe to use on trees.

- **Red Spider Mites**

Description: Red spider mites are a tiny pest and even though they are smaller than aphids, they are much faster moving and can kill a plant at an accelerated rate. Once red spider mites settle on a tree, they get to work very quickly.

The main problem with these types of mites is their size. Because they're so small they are very easy to overlook and not notice. Only if one is very close to the leaves can they see the little mites moving and even then, it's when one knows what they're looking for.

Symptoms: The first indication that enthusiasts normally see that there's a problem is that the leaves on their bonsais start to get yellow and brown blotches on the leaves of their bonsai.

Cure: The treatment for these types of mites is normally with a pesticide because they spread so rapidly. It is best to quarantine your bonsai to prevent further spread and then treat as best as you can. If you catch the infection early and treat the mites rapidly, your bonsai should recover to its full health.

- **White Grubs**

Description: Most pests target the top of the trees but grubs, on the other hand, go straight for the root systems of trees and larger plants. This means that the root systems of bonsais are susceptible to the larvae of several different beetles known as grubs. And, unfortunately, there is no way of knowing there is a problem until the problems start to manifest themselves above ground.

Symptoms: Because grubs attack the roots, the tree will seem healthy at first, but it will start to seem more sickly over time. Pay attention to the leaves of your bonsai and if you notice that the leaves are starting to wilt regardless of what you do, and if you can't see any other problems on the surface, then the problem may be lying underground. There may be some evidence of adult beetle attacks on your bonsai if the leaves have been eaten. You can differentiate a beetle's bite marks from those of caterpillars or snails by the fact that beetle's eat notches into leaves instead of in circular patterns. The indicative U-shape holes are normally created by beetles.

Cure: If your bonsai is looking unhealthy and there is evidence of this, it's best to remove the tree from its pot and inspect the roots. It will be easy to spot any grubs in the root system and they can easily be removed by hand.

- *Scale*

Description: Scale pests are insects that come in a variety of shapes, sizes, and colors. These insects range from white to yellow to black and even though they move around a lot when they're younger, they tend to find one place that they're comfortable in when they're nearing adulthood and then hunker down and dig into the flesh of the plant they are on.

Once they have burrowed through the protective layers of the plant, they start to drink the sap, but unlike other insects, these stay put and don't move once they have found their spot. **Symptoms**: Because they take up permanent residence on one site and have a shiny covering, they resemble scales.

Cure: The best treatment for these types of infections is to physically remove them by hand. Because the insects don't move, they are easy to scrape off with your fingernails and then rinse off. Once you have removed all of the scales it's advisable to apply some bonsai cut cream to the areas to prevent infection.

- *Snails and Slugs*

Description: Everyone has probably seen slugs and snails in the gardens at some point or another and these pests can be very destructive to plant life. They thrive in damp conditions and are most common during the warm, rainy seasons.

Symptoms: Even though they are very slow-moving, they are able to strip an entire bonsai of its leaves in a matter of hours.

Cure: The best treatment against these pests is to go out at night with a flashlight and search for them. Because they are mostly nocturnal, they are very active at night and they like to move around more in cooler temperatures, so they will come out of hiding. If you suspect that there may be a problem in your garden or around your bonsais, then a bit of nocturnal hunting may do the trick to protect your bonsais.

- **Laniger aphid and white cochineal**

Description: They are small insects that develop at the expense of the plant, surrounding themselves with a white waxy substance and feeding on the sap.

Symptoms: White and woolly formations wrap around the petioles of the leaves and the divergence of the branches, weakening the plant.

Cure: Use Croneton or Compron on the soil, or water with Ekamet or Proposcur at 0.15%.

- **Black aphid**

Description: It is an insect that lives in colonies, spreading especially in spring and creating blackish formations attached to sheets and flowers. This slows down the development of the plant in the affected areas.

Symptoms: Dark windings hit the shoots and stretch to the leaves and flowers.

Cure: Use Croneton and Primor without affecting the flowers.

- **Cochineal**

Description: It is an insect that feeds on the sap of plants, injecting a chemical substance inside that causes an abundant secretion of sugars.

Symptoms: In the lower part of the leaves dark-colored folds are created.

Care: It would sometimes be sufficient to remove the animals from the plant with a simple stick, however, the use of Primor or 0.2% Aphisan, sprayed on the plant, or Croneton poured into the ground is recommended.

- **Phylloxeraradicicol**

Description: It is a female aphid of small size, green or yellow-brown, which lays a large number of eggs and attacks the roots of plants.

Symptoms: The plant tends to turn yellow and deteriorate. Looking at the roots or the earth, one can notice small gray-white ball formations.

Cure: Pour on the ground of Croneton or a solution of Metasystox or Alphos.

- **Whitefly or Aleuroids**

Description: The whitefly is a white insect whose larvae, hidden under the leaves, feed on the sap of the plant, forcing it to emit various sugary productions. It mainly affects plants such as Lantana and Segerezia.

Symptoms: The leaves begin to turn yellow at the bottom and weaken.

Care: The use of products such as Folithion, Ambush, or Undene is recommended.

- **Lice or aphids**

Description: Lice and aphids are insects that live in rather large groups, attaching themselves to the trunk and leaves to suck the sap. Some species are equipped with wings and, moving from plant to plant, they also favor the spread of viruses. *Symptoms:* Insect groups cover leaves and buds that weaken and decay.

Cure: There may be enough water to remove them. Otherwise use Primor or Croneton, or spray with Parexan or another spray.

- **Red spider or garden mite**

Description: They are small red, yellow or brown spiders that make their nests on the leaves on the branches. They attack both fruit trees and plants of other species.

Symptoms: The leaves are wrapped in very thin cobwebs on which it is possible to notice animals with a lens. Over time the leaves turn yellow and weaken.

Cure: We recommend using Tetagril on the ground, or spraying the plant with special Lizetan or Metasystox R, particularly suitable against these insects.

Plant parasites are caused by conditions of the particular weakness of the plant that facilitate the spread of diseases.

- *Chlorosis*

Description: It is a disease due to a lack of iron or excess calcium in the soil. Factors that prevent easy absorption of mineral substances cause a serious deficiency of chlorophyll inside the plant.

Symptoms: The leaves begin to turn yellow, but leave the ribs green, and wither.

Cure: Before watering, pour Fetrilon or Sequestrene into the right amount.

- *Sooty mold*

Description: They are fungi that affect the bonsai in the trunk, in the leaves and the branches, giving rise to dark incrustations. Mushrooms often feed on sugary substances caused by the passage of aphids and above all are favored by high humidity and poor ventilation.

Symptoms: Dark-colored spots or sooty areas are created in the affected areas.

Cure: We recommend the use of Cupravit or Baymat, or in any case of any product with copper oxychloride.

- *Radical rot*

Description - Symptoms: The best treatment for this problem is prevention. It is best to not overwater your bonsai and also keep the ground in the pot clear of any fallen foliage. Sometimes, infected leaves can drop onto the soil and infect it with a fungus, so it's best to remove them when you notice some leaves have died and fallen off. It is also necessary to ensure that your tree is an area that is well-ventilated and has decent exposure to sunlight.

If you suspect that your bonsai may have root rot, it is best to remove your bonsai from its pot and prune away all of the infected roots. This may or not work because of the severity of the fungal spread, but it is worth the try. Once all of the infected roots have been pruned, the tree needs to be planted in fast-draining soil.

The roots rot mainly for two reasons: Excessive fertilization, which causes damage and necrosis, and an excessively abundant watering, which causes water to stagnate in the soil.

Root rot is a problem that all bonsais face because they spend their lives in pots. This problem is caused by a fungus because of poor drainage in the pot. Plants and trees that are planted in the ground don't usually face this problem but it is a risk for any potted tree or plant.

As soon as the water starts to back up and the roots sit in unnecessary fluid, they become much softer and at risk for fungal infections. If roots turn brown and take on a mushy-like consistency, the tree won't be able to draw up water and nutrients any longer and the tree will inevitably die.

It is important to note that not all fungi in roots are bad things and root rot shouldn't be confused with the white fungus that grows in the roots of pine trees because that fungus is absolutely essential to the pine trees' survival.

The plant weakens and begins to perish, due to the Tadice's inability to forfeit nourishment, the leaves take on a dark color.

Cure:

Severe root rot can be treated with Lime Sulfur, a broad-acting fungicide, and it may be able to kill the fungus. If there are roots still strong enough to heal, there still may be a chance of survival. But it's definitely best not to let it get to this point and rather prevent it from occurring altogether.

It is good to cut the sick and already dead roots and leave the healthy ones in a solution of Benomyl or Orthocid, after having cleaned them well from the ground.

Kiplantate the bonsai in a pot with new soil, keeping the soil watered and moist fertilizing should be practiced only after 2 months.

- **Powdery mildew or Spaerotheca**

Description: They are also fungi that affect the plant in particular conditions of temperature and ventilation. Their propagation is facilitated by the particular heat and humidity, so it is good to be particularly careful in the summer.

Symptoms: Powdery mildew creates a whitish powder-like substance on the front of the leaves and in the other affected points, gradually weakening the plant.

Cure: To eliminate powdery mildew in a short time, you can use any fungicide or even a KB solution of micronized sulfur to be administered every 15 days.

- **False powdery mildew**

Description: It is a mushroom similar to the previous one, even if it manifests itself differently way. It is favored by inadequate conditions of temperature and humidity.

Symptoms: It determines a gray moldy substance in the lower part of the leaves, while it turns yellow the upper one, staining some points of gray.

Cure: Use Bayleton or CupravitBlu, spraying it in the relevant points, transporting the bonsai to a well-ventilated place

- ***Virosis***

Description: These are all the diseases caused by the spread of viruses which, however, are still not easily identifiable today and which often occur in a deleterious way for plants.

The virus spreads easily or through insects, or due to infected tools, or in any circumstance in which some wounds of the tree can be affected, such as in the case of grafts, pruning, etc.

Symptoms: The symptoms are various and are not always recognizable in a short time. In the most common cases, these are streaks of various colors that are highlighted on the leaves; regardless of the symptoms the fate of the plant is however probably sealed.

Cure: Unfortunately, there are few remedies after a plant has been affected.

You can only try to make sure that the infection does not expand, moving the plant away. Above all, however, it is recommended to prevent virosis by fighting animal parasites and keeping tools clean.

PROBLEMS DUE TO THE ENVIRONMENT

Bonsai must always be placed in an environment suitable for its needs. Each species requires a certain amount of light, humidity, temperature, which must be guaranteed overtime for the good health of the plant. Let's see together how to give our bonsai the optimal environment.

There are multiple things that you may need to consider when dealing with growing your bonsai but the three most important factors that you need to keep in mind (regardless of where you are in the world) are light, humidity, and temperature.

If you have locally sourced your seeds it is advisable to keep your bonsai outdoors because it's in an environment that it will thrive in, but if you are growing a non-indigenous bonsai, then it may be necessary to keep your bonsai indoors to better control the factors it is exposed to.

Temperature

Most bonsais prefer slightly warmer climates during their growing periods and they will require slightly warmer temperatures in the spring and summer months. It is perfectly healthy if you wish for your bonsai to go dormant in the colder months but during the spring and summer, it is best to keep your bonsai at temperatures between 68 and 86 degrees F. (20 to 30 degrees Celsius).

Keeping your bonsai at this temperature will allow for it to stay healthy while it's indoors and since it's indoors there will be a lower chance of pests and other infections attacking your bonsai, provided the ventilation, watering, and fertilizing are occurring well.

It is good to always keep in mind the temperature of the original place of the plant and try to recreate it also in our apartment.

Plants are classified into two groups, depending on their origin and needs: Tropical plants and subtropical plants.

Tropical plants need during the day temperature between 18 and 24 degrees Celsius - 64.4-75,2 F.; at night it is better not to drop below 15-16 degrees Celsius – 60 F..

The subtropical plants, on the other hand, do not bear a too hot climate, and I prefer minimum temperatures in winter between 5 and 12 degrees Celsius - 41-53,6 F..

Not respecting these needs of the plant means causing them serious damage.

In general, the cold causes a slowdown in growth, chlorosis, cracking of the branches or the trunk, the death of the leaves, even the death of all the bonsai.

It also happens if the temperature is too hot with the risk the plant ends up drying out.

We, therefore, recommend keeping bonsai in a suitable place: Tropical plants are usually placed on heating sources or as close as possible, to exploit their heat throughout the day.

At night it is good to take them to a slightly cooler place, to cause a natural temperature, drop of 5-6 degrees Celsius – 41-42.8 F..

Subtropical plants are more suitable for winter gardens, cool rooms, or in the corridor.

Also, in this case, it is recommended to provide a slight drop in temperature during the night by bringing the plant near the window or in a cooler place.

It is good, however, that the temperature changes are not excessive.

If you intend to place the plants in the open air for the summer, it will be better not to expose them directly to sunlight, they will necessarily be collected at home when the night temperature starts to drop below I degrees.

Light

Plants, as we know, have a great need for light to be able to start the process of photosynthesis, but in this case, too it is good not to exceed.

The excess of light in especially if the plant is not used to it can cause the discoloration of the leaves and a consequent weakening of the plant.

We, therefore, recommend keeping the bonsai in a bright place, without it being directly exposed to the sun's rays.

If you are planning on keeping your bonsai inside because you know you will spend more time with it like that, you will need to find a way to get it to receive enough UV light.

In the home it is often necessary to use artificial light to integrate the one coming from outside; in this case, it is better to avoid normal incandescent bulbs because they emit light too different from the solar one.

One of the greatest difficulties of keeping a tropical bonsai indoors is ensuring that it is exposed to enough light with a high enough intensity.

We recommend quartz and iodine lamps and fluorescent tubes for aquariums.

Trees are resilient and they won't die immediately if their ideal conditions aren't met, but their health will deteriorate over time. Therefore, it is much better to ensure that your bonsai has enough light from the very beginning.

Placing your bonsai in front of a window that receives a lot of sunlight will greatly benefit your bonsai in the long run, so choosing the right window is paramount to your bonsai's overall success. Some windows may seem light enough but they may not receive the correct amount of UV ray concentration needed for a healthy bonsai. Windows situated at the east or west of the house will be ideal because they will receive the morning or afternoon sun.

That being said, this is for bonsais from tropical climates, and some trees can function with indirect light, so adequate research is always necessary.

Humidity

Some trees thrive in humidity, while others prefer drier climates. But most bonsais function fairly well with increased humidity levels because they can draw from the moisture in the air. The only challenge with this is that some bonsais may require humidity levels that are higher than those in your house, especially if you have air-conditioners or heaters running.

You may think that you will need to buy a humidifier for your bonsai, but a simple tray of water next to the tree can create some vapor as it stands in the sunlight or a regular misting with a spray bottle is also sufficient. As long as your bonsai receives water vapor from the air, it will grow very well.

As it is easy to guess, two factors can come into play by damaging the plant, if not kept under constant control: The humidity of the air and the watering.

Most bonsai need a humidity of between 40 and 50%.

If the bonsai is placed in a too dry place, the plant evaporates more water than it manages to forfeit from the roots, causing a decrease in growth and risking the leaves, branches and trunk to dry out.

On the contrary, on the other hand, if the humidity is excessive, there is a danger of a general weakening of the plant, of the spread of parasitic diseases such as fungi, up to the possibility that the whole plant will rot. As we said, watering also plays an important role and should be practiced in moderation.

Excess water with bad drainage in the soil facilitates root rot, fungi and pests. It also decreases the speed of development of the plant, causing it asphyxiation and heaviness.

It is therefore better to water often, but in moderate quantities, rather than rarely in large quantities. It is also good to make sure that the water does not stagnate in the pot, but has an easy outlet thanks to the drainage holes.

DISEASES DUE TO EXCESS OR LACK OF NUTRIENTS

Plants can also get sick when the soil does not adequately contain all the elements necessary for nourishment. The bonsai highlights particular symptoms that can become real diseases if you don't try to live the problem immediately with adequate fertilizer. Often, then, the lack of water causes serious damage to leaves and flowers, such as the drying out of the log edges, deformation and fall of the shoots, etc. On the contrary, too much water prevents the soil from breathing, causing root rot.

Now we will examine the nutrients that can cause damage to the plant if they are not present in the necessary quantity.

- **Nitrogen**

    If the soil contains an excessive amount of nitrogen, the tree tends to accelerate its development speed, but this causes a weakening of the plant and a lower ability to defend against disease and cold. If instead the percentage of nitrogen is lower, the development slows down and the vegetative cycle is shortened, to the detriment of leaves and shoots.

- **Boron**

    The lack of boron damages the leaves which weaken, drying out easily.

    The plant deteriorates and does not grow.

- **Iron**

    Iron in small quantities causes the leaves to turn yellow and weaken the plant.

- **Phosphorus**

The lack of phosphorus in the soil causes the plant to stop developing, giving the leaves a bronze color and making them leathery.

- **Magnesium**

    The lack of magnesium in the soil gives the leaves red and chlorosis coloring.

- **Potassium**

    When the plant lacks the right amount of potassium, serious damage to the leaves occurs. They begin to curl on the edges and turn dark and rot; the whole plant suffers, weakening its defenses.

- **Zinc**

    The plant slows down its development, with the consequence that the leaves remain small and thin and easily affected by chlorosis.

INJURIES AND WOUNDS

Let's talk now about how-to bring relief to the plant in case of injuries caused by diseases or by bad use of tools.

It is first of all important to try to prevent the possibility of injury by keeping the bonsai in a sheltered place, where there is no risk of damage. Also, it is always good to keep the tools in good condition and, during pruning, make a clean and flat cut, to limit the extent of the wound to a minimum.

Plants have a great natural healing ability, however, always good to help them by applying waxes and pastes that contain healing hormones such as Lac balsam or other products readily available on the market.

In case there are dead or infected parts, it is good to remove them immediately, in order to facilitate the recovery of the plant.

Furthermore, during the vegetative period and especially when it is very hot, the plant must be followed in a particular way because it is more active and more willing to infections.

CHAPTER 6 - CONTAINERS AND TOOLS

The choice of the container can compromise or enhance the overall harmony of bonsai creation. An ideal container can bring out a plant without particular value, hiding its defects and highlighting its most peculiar characteristics.

Usually, they are made in porcelain or terracotta and it is not uncommon to find vitrified models on the outside.

However, the containers on the market offer such a variety, of colors and sizes, that the choice is not always easy. However, some rules can help us.

The suitable dimensions depend on those of the bonsai: The pot must be at least two-thirds of the height of the trunk and the height should not be less than the thickness of the trunk.

As for the color, we usually tend to create particular contrasts between the container and the tree, as required by the principle of asymmetric balancing. So, for trees with dark foliage, vases with light colors will be used mostly and vice versa.

This rule is however subject to the taste of the bonsai artist, who may deem preferable, which among other things, in some cases is necessary for a good overall object. Each style prefers a certain shape of the container:

- **Moyogi:** Oval, shallow, round, shallow and rectangular containers can be used.
- **Chokkan:** Shallow, oval and rectangular square pots are to be used.
- **Shakan:** Shallow, round, shallow and rectangular shapes are recommended.

- **Kengai:** Containers must be very deep rounds to allow the tree to develop properly alongside the pot.
- **Sokan:** The containers can be oval and round low
- **Sankan:** The recommended containers are the low shapeless ones.
- **Vahudachi:** Low round, rectangular and low shapeless vases are used.
- **Ikada:** Oval and low-form ones are suitable.
- **Netsuranari:** Shapeless low vessels are recommended.
- **Vose-ue:** The containers must be oval, rectangular or low-form.
- **Hokidachi:** Oval, shallow square, low round and shallow, rectangular and low shapeless containers are to be used.
- **Fukinagashi:** The recommended shapes are oval, shallow square, low round and shallow and rectangular.
- **Bunjingi:** Low and shallow round pots are recommended.
- **Ishitsuki:** The oval, low round and rectangular vases fit.
- **Saikei and Bonkei:** It is preferable to use low oval and rectangular vases, even if all those containers that enhance the general composition are suitable.
- **Han-Kengai:** Use deep or very deep square or very deep round vases.

The use of containers with feet is preferable, because keeping the vase raised concerning the support surface, it allows better air circulation and more easy expulsion of water.

Often the bonsai are placed on special wooden display tables or mobile shelves. The latter, which is useful for moving the plant when necessary, can also be easily built on their own.

ARRANGEMENT OF BONSAI IN THE CONTAINER

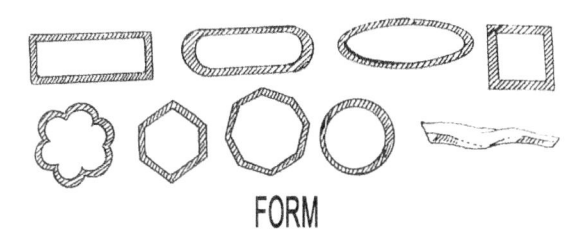

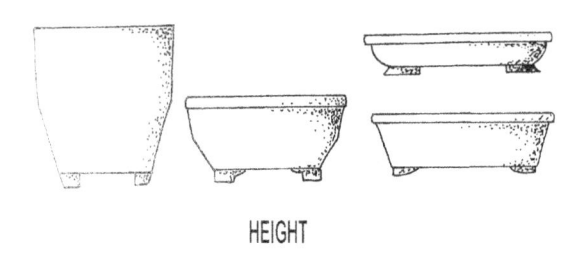

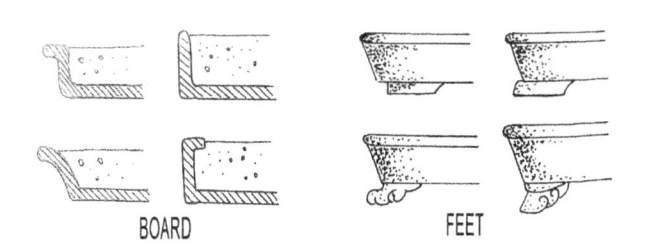

FORM

HEIGHT

BOARD   **FEET**

After having seen the variety of containers, let's now see together some general advice on which arrangement is best to give the bonsai in their container.

To facilitate the exposure, it is good to make a first distinction between the front and the back of the bonsai. The front is visible to the observer.

It will be necessary, therefore, to choose as the front of the bonsai that part that does not have branches directed towards the observer, to give an orderly and accurate impression to the composition.

Usually, then the roots that emerge from the ground are also placed towards the front, to give an idea of greater stability to the whole plant.

It is also essential to distinguish between straight trunk trees, leaning trunk trees and groups of trees.

Each of these cases will follow different rules:

- **Straight trunk trees:** if your style includes trees with a straight trunk, you will need to arrange the trunk so that it is moved a little back from the center of the pot and slightly inclined towards you. This will result in a lively look, accentuating the shape of the canopy relative to the trunk
- **Tree with leaning trunk:** The inclination of the tree must always be oriented right to left or the other way around. In case the tree leans to the right, you will have to move the base of the trunk to the left of the container. Otherwise, instead, you have to move the trunk to the right of the container. Also, for this group of trees, it is advisable to bring a slight inclination towards the front
- **Groups of trees:** If you have chosen trees that have double or multiple trunks coming from the same root, these will always be arranged in the center of the container. If instead the trees are autonomous from each other and you want to make a composition, they can be arranged in a more varied way.

In this regard, however, more information can be found in the chapter dedicated to group styles.

BONSAI TOOLS

Let's now describe the main tools to be used in the maintenance and transformation of bonsai. For those who are preparing to start growing a bonsai, the following tools are needed:

1. A plastic or metal watering can equip with replaceable onions with a flat and inclined face. The first provides a strong enough jet, useful for watering leaves and foliage. The second is to be used to water the soil as it makes the water flow more gently.
2. A pair of elongated bonsai pruning shears. The length of these elongated allows you to work inside the foliage very easily.
3. A pair of wide scissors, useful for truncating large roots. A bonsai hacksaw can also be used for this purpose.

4. A pair of concave shears, useful for cutting branches to obtain a section as regular as possible, facilitating wound healing.
5. Mesh in thin mesh to be placed over the drainage holes, to prevent lumps of earth from coming out.
6. Aluminum wire to wrap branches and trunk, in case you want to change its shape.
7. A small wire cutter to cut the wire without injuring the bark.
8. A stick or a paperclip to clean the roots from the ground and separate them during repotting.
9. A rake to level the ground.
10. A broom to clean.

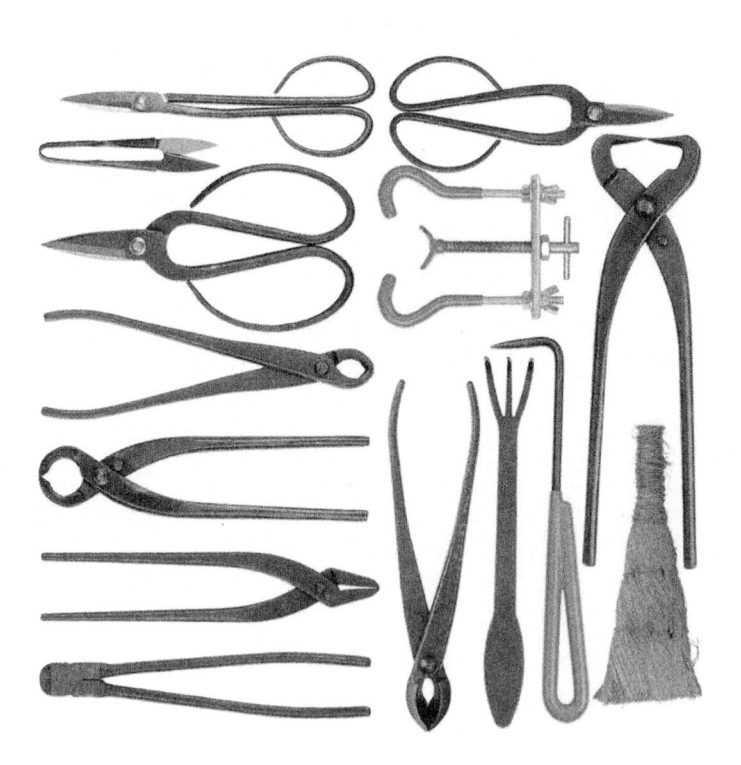

It is essential to remember to carefully clean each tool after use to avoid the spread of germs or diseases. For this purpose, it is possible to find types of disinfectants for tools on the market.

CHAPTER 7 - TIPS AND INFORMATION

Keeping a bonsai may be something that excites and frightens you at the same time and since there are so many things you need to remember, it may feel overwhelming. But it is important for you as an enthusiast to work with your bonsai in the ways that you feel fit, and also keep in mind that you don't always have to keep an eye on it. Some enthusiasts are worried about leaving their bonsai for a few days because they're worried something may go wrong during that period, but there is little risk.

If you are going away for a few days, then it's fine to give your bonsai slightly more water than you normally would. A single watering that's slightly more than normal isn't going to hurt the tree, and just ensure that you have fertilized it too before leaving (if you are going away in the summer months). But, if you are leaving for slightly longer periods of time, then it's best to give the bonsai to someone you trust with a set of instructions on how to water and feed it.

When the holiday season arrives, you will face the problem of how to behave with bonsai, where to leave it, whom to leave it, etc. Always comes up.

The ideal would be to have someone to whom to entrust him who is able to replace our care for the necessary period, however, this is not always possible. In the event that the absence is short-lived, lasting up to a week, then the bonsai can be left alone, even if it is necessary to prepare a suitable place to keep it moist all the time. It will be sufficient to bury the pot inside a larger container that has a layer of wet peat. Otherwise, you can create a small greenhouse with a transparent plastic bag inside which to insert the pot. The bag will be closed over the bonsai after it has been watered abundantly. It is also necessary to drill holes in the plastic to circulate the air while maintaining the necessary humidity inside.

For longer periods, a connection can be made between a container full of water, placed higher up, and the bonsai pot using a tube that slowly brings water to a wedge planted in the soil.

To obtain the same result in an easier way, a simple woolen thread can be used instead of the tube and the wedge impregnating the water with the thread, it will slowly let it drop on the ground.

However, even in this case, a person's assistance would be needed to check that everything is going well and to solve any problems that could arise.

There may be times that your bonsai gets hurt because of a mistake you made or because something happened to it. Remember that accidents happen but you will be able to solve many of these problems with the correct tools. Before starting to grow your bonsai, it's advisable to get a bonsai kit so you can have the clippers, wire, cut-cream, and bonsai scissors. If you have these items, taking care of your bonsai won't be difficult.

If your bonsai gets a damaged trunk, treat it as you would a wound on yourself. Place the cut-cream on the wound and wrap it with bonsai tape and plastic wrap to protect it from infection. This method can be used from anything from grafts to a trunk that's been split.

The final tip is to trust yourself and always do your research on the bonsais that you are keeping. You won't know everything about bonsais in the beginning, but you are able to know a lot about the bonsais you are currently keeping or interested in growing in the future.

1) Watering by subtracting the bonsai pot in a moist soil; 2) Watering through a wire of wool connected to a basin of water; 3) Greenhouse made with plastic bag

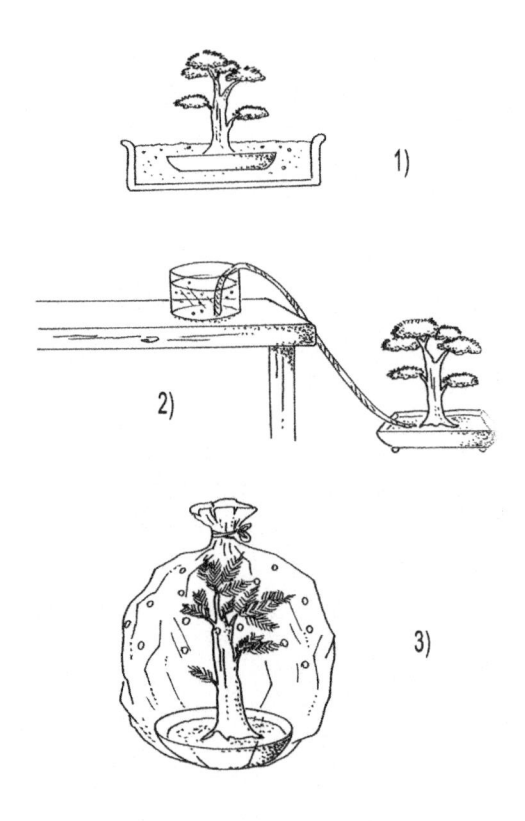

1)

2)

3)

CHAPTER 8 – 54-PLANTS DATASHEETS

We now give a list of the main characteristics of each type of bonsai plant, indispensable for taking care of all the processing phases.

In case you are interested in a bonsai whose name is not in the list, know that the indications you find for a certain species can also be applied to any other plant in the same family.

ARALIA MING (POLYSCIAS FRUCTICOSA)

Family: Araliaceae

Description: Aralia Ming is a large shrub from Polynesia and tropical Asia. It is characterized by a wrinkled golden-green trunk, dense branches and tender leaves, supported by a very elongated petiole.

Environment and exposure: It can be kept next to a very bright window, even exposed to direct sunlight, if these are not too strong. In summer it can be taken out in a sunny place, while in winter it prefers an environment with temperatures between 18 and 20 degrees Celsius- 64.4-68 F..

Watering: The Aralia Ming must be kept always humid, with continuous watering and spraying often also on the leaves.

Fertilization: It is recommended to fertilize from March to September with liquid fertilizer, every 2 weeks. In the winter stasis, on the other hand, you only have to fertilize once every 4-5 weeks.

Repotting: It is good to repot at least once every two during the beginning of spring, to shorten and cut the roots.

Soil: The ideal soil consists of a mixture of clay for 1/4, of peat for 2/4, and of sand for the remaining 1/4.

Pruning: The branches can always be sprouted or cut throughout the year the shoots instead they are topped in groups of 2-3 pairs when they have reached 5-6 pairs. It is also good to eliminate too large leaves.

Binding: The Aralia Ming has a structure that is not suitable for binding, both because of the shape it naturally assumes and because the practice is not very effective.

Multiplication: Multiplication with the cutting method is recommended.

AZALEA (AZALEA INDICA)

Family: Ericaceae

Description: It is a subtropical shrub from East Asia, characterized by colorful flowers and bright green leaves.

Flowering: In the period from spring to autumn, flowers bloom can be white, pink, red, orange, or purple.

Environment and exposure: All year round it can be kept near a bright and ventilated window. In summer you can take it out without ever exposing it to the sun. In winter it prefers temperatures between 5 and 10 degrees Celsius – 41-50 F..

Watering: For the summer period it is good to water continuously and in abundance. In winter it is sufficient to keep the soil quite humid.

Fertilization: It can be fertilized only in summer, with liquid fertilizer, administered once every 2 weeks, completely stopping for the winter.

Repotting: It is necessary to repot once every 2-3 years, after flowering, cutting and sprouting too long roots.

Soil: The most suitable mixture for Azalea consists of clay for 1/5, peat for 2/5 and sand for the other 2/5.

Pruning: Branches can always be cut; on the contrary, the shoots are topped to decrease the number of leaves from 6 pairs to 2-3 pairs. Also, wilted flowers must be eliminated to allow the plant to develop seeds.

Binding: It is possible to practice it on branches and shoots that are sufficiently lignified, however particular attention is necessary due to the fragile structure of the plant.

Multiplication: The most suitable is the multiplication by cutting.

BAMBOO (BAMBUSA HUMILIS)

Family: Araminaceae

Description: It is a plant native to China and India, characterized by a hollow, gnarled and elongated stem. The leaves are pointed and light green in color.

Environment and exposure: All year round it can be housed near a bright window, although it is recommended to take it outside in the summer, without placing it in the sun. For winter the ideal temperature is between 15 and 18 degrees Celsius – 59-64 F..

Watering: Watering must be regular and abundant throughout the year to keep the soil constantly humid.

Fertilization: Fertilization is recommended only in the period from March to September, using liquid fertilizer, once every 2 weeks.

Repotting: Repotting always in spring every one or two years, depending on the age of the plant, by shortening and cutting the roots.

Soil: The ideal mixture consists of 2/5 of clay, 2/5 of sand, and 1/5 of peat.

Pruning: It is recommended to carefully trim the shoots, to reduce the size of the bonsai.

Binding: The structure of the Bamboo makes the application of the metal wire inadvisable.

Multiplication: Among the various methods, the one that obtains the best results is the multiplication by cutting.

BEECH (FAGUS SYLVATICA)

Family: fagaceae

Description: large tree native to areas of southern Europe and western Asia. It is characterized by a gray and smooth trunk, by thin and abundant branches and by bright green oval leaves.

Environment and exposure: Beech should be kept in a very bright area, near a sunny window. In summer it can be taken outside, in the half-light, or the sun if this is not too strong. In winter, winter, the temperature must be between 12 and 15 degrees Celsius - 53-59 F

Watering: it is advisable to water abundantly and regularly throughout the year, preventing the soil from drying out.

Fertilization: for the whole period from March to October, it is necessary to fertilize once every 3 weeks. In the winter period instead, it is sufficient to give fertilizer every 4 or 5 weeks.

Repotting: repotting should be practiced once every year, during the beginning of spring, by cutting and shortening too long roots.

Soil: the most suitable mixture for beech, is made up of clay, peat and cage in equal proportions

Pruning: the branches can be pruned in spring and early autumn. The shoots are topped to decrease the number of leaves from 5-6 pairs to 2-3.

Binding: it is important to remember that as regards the Beech it is preferable to practice the binding after the shoots are cut, on well-lignified branches and twigs.

Multiplication: methods by seed and by cuttings are recommended.

BIRCH (BETULA NIGRA)

Family: Betulaceae

Description: Shrub native to cold temperate regions, characterized by the stem and thin branches and by pointed and serrated leaves.

Environment and exposure: Birch must be kept in a very bright and ventilated place. For the summer period, it is recommended to take it outside without exposing it too much to the sun. In winter it is better to maintain a temperature between 10 and 15 degrees Celsius – 50-59 F..

Watering: Throughout the period between April and October it is advisable to water regularly, keeping the soil constantly humid. In winter it is possible to decrease the doses of water while preventing the soil from drying out too much.

Fertilization: Fertilization should be practiced only in the period between May and September, distributing fertilizer, preferably liquid, once every 3 weeks.

Repotting: The most suitable time for repotting is once every two years, at the beginning of spring, just before the buds appear.

Soil: The most suitable mixture to meet the needs of birch must be rather acidic, therefore we recommend a mixture of 1/4 of clay, 2/4 of peat, and 1/4 of sand.

Pruning: It is better to prune the branches in the period just before the growth of the shoots; even if the operation guarantees good results throughout the year. The shoots should be sprouted from 5-6 pairs of leaves to 1-2 pairs.

Binding: Summer is the most suitable time to apply metal wire. It should be remembered, however, to pay particular attention to the degree of robustness of the branches and shoots.

Multiplication: Birch can be multiplied by seed and cutting methods.

BOX-TREE (BUXUS HARLANDII)

Family: Buxaceae

Description: Boxtree is an evergreen shrub characteristic of the Far East and Mediterranean coasts. The thick foliage and the abundance of branches have highlighted it as an excellent plant for hedges. Its branches are often cut in a particular way to obtain geometric shapes or other types of figures.

Flowering: Small flowers develop in the winter period from November to January.

Environment and exposure: The box-tree needs a bright and cool place so we recommend placing it near a window throughout the year. If in summer you want to take it outside, from May to September, it is good to leave it in a place protected from direct sun. In winter it is good to keep the temperature between 10 and 15 degrees Celsius – 50-59 F..

Watering: Watering must be very abundant in summer and repeated every time the soil dries. In winter, it is best to decrease the intensity to a few times a week, depending on the needs of the plant.

Fertilization: Fertilization must be practiced for the whole period from spring to autumn. We recommend a liquid fertilizer for bonsai, every twenty days or so. If the bonsai is placed in a warm place even in winter, it can be fertilized once every 35-40 days.

Repotting: It is recommended to practice it every two years, at the arrival of spring, cutting and shortening all the roots.

Soil: It is recommended to make a mixture of 2/5 of the earth for bonsai or clay, 2/5 of sand, and 1/5 of peat.

Pruning: The branches can be pruned throughout the year. When clusters of leaves are born, it is recommended that the number be reduced to two or three pairs.

Binding: Possible throughout the year.

Multiplication: We recommend using the cutting method.

BUGANVILLEA (BOUGAINVILLEA GLABRA)

Family: nictaginaceae

Description: it is a shrub from the areas of Brazil and southern America, characterized by long, thorny branches and smooth, light green-green leaves.

Flowering: in the period from June to September it develops small flowers covered with bracts with very bright colors.

Environment and exposure: all year round it can be positioned next to a window in an illuminated and ventilated area. In the period from May to September, it can also be placed outside in a sunny position. In winter we recommend a temperature between 10 and 15 degrees Celsius – 50-59 F.

Watering: for the summer period, the soil must be watered regularly to keep it moist, but in moderation so as not to risk dropping the leaves. For the winter, the soil will be left completely dry before supplying new water.

Fertilizing: especially in the fertilization period: yes, in summer, by administering fertilizer every 15-20 days. In winter we will limit ourselves to fertilizing once every 4-5 weeks.

Repotting: repotting should be practiced once every 2 or 3 years, at the arrival of spring, by cutting and sprouting the overdeveloped roots.

Soil: the most suitable mixture consists of 2/5 of clay, 2/5 of peat and 1/5 of sand.

Pruning: we recommend pruning the branches and shoots all year round, except during the flowering period.

Multiplication: the most suitable method is that of cutting, to be practiced in spring.

CAMELLIA JAPONICA (CAMELIA JAPONICA)

Family: Theaceae

Description: Camellia japonica is native to China and Japan. It is characterized by a slightly silvery trunk and foliage with leathery, dark green leaves. It can reach a height of 3 to 8 yards.

Flowering: From December to March abundant white, pink, or red or red flowers bloom.

Environment and exposure: It must be maintained throughout the year in a well-ventilated and bright place, possibly near a window. In summer it is possible to take it outside from March to September, placing it in an area of the penumbra. The preferable temperature in winter fluctuates between 6 and 12 degrees Celsius – 42-56 F..

Watering: Camellia needs constantly moist soil in summer, while in winter it can be watered more rarely.

Fertilization: It is recommended to fertilize in the period between flowering and the end of autumn, using liquid fertilizer every 2 weeks.

Repotting: It is necessary to repot in the spring, once every 2-4 years, cutting the roots.

Soil: The mixture must be 1/5 of clay, 2/5 of peat, and 2/5 of sand.

Pruning: Pruning the branches after flowering, reducing the number of leaves of the shoots to a number of 2 or 3.

Binding: The branches can always be tied, with the exception of the flowering ones. Sprouts, on the other hand, should only be tied towards the end of summer when they are better strengthened.

Multiplication: It is recommended by cuttings, although not always of sure success.

CHERRY OF THE ANTILLES (MALPIGHIA COCCIGERA)

Family: Malpighiaceae

Description: It is an evergreen shrub from the Antilles, the leaves, thorny, have a bright green color.

Blooming: In the period from June to August, it produces small pinkish-white flowers.

Environment and exposure: Throughout the year it can be kept indoors, near a window, in a bright and ventilated place, however, it cannot stand the direct sun. In winter it is recommended to keep the temperature around 18-20 degrees Celsius – 64-68 F..

Watering: Throughout the year it is best to keep the soil constantly humid. In fact, even in winter, the plant is kept in a warm environment

Fertilization: Throughout the year the fertilizer will be given once every two weeks, except in winter, when 4- weeks will pass between one administration and another.

Repotting: We recommend always repotting in the spring, once a year, or once every two years, popping up and cutting the roots.

Soil: The ideal soil consists of a mixture of 2/4 of clay, 1 / of peat and 1/4 of sand.

Pruning: The shoots must be pruned in order to reduce the number of leaves to one or two pairs, while the branches can always be pruned.

Binding: Branches and shoots can always be tied as long as they are strong enough not to risk breaking.

Multiplication: The plant is suitable for multiplication by cuttings or by seed.

CHINESE ELM (ULMUS PARVIFOLIA)

Family: ulmaceae

Description: it is a large tree from areas of China, it has a light-colored trunk and rather thin branches, rich in oval leaves, light green and shaped. If allowed to grow in its areas of origin, it reaches a height of twenty yards.

Environment and exposure: throughout the year it can be kept indoors, next to a bright and sunny window. For the summer period, it is advisable to take it outside, also placing it in the sun, if this is not too intense. In winter, given the great strength of the Elm, it can be kept both at warm temperatures (10-20 degrees celsius - 50-68 F.) and cooler (5-10 degrees celsius).

Watering: in summer it is good to water continuously and in abundance, avoiding that the soil remains too dry. During the winter, if it "winters in the heat", it will be watered as in summer, otherwise use more moderate and occasional doses of water, while keeping the soil moist.

Fertilization: for the entire period from March to September we recommend fertilizing once every 2 weeks. In winter the use of fertilizer will decrease to once every 4-5 weeks.

Repotting: repotting should be practiced once every two years, when spring arrives, sprouting and cutting the roots that have developed too much.

Soil: the ideal soil for growing Elm is made up of a mixture of 2/4 clay, 1/4 sand and 1/4 peat.

Pruning: branches and shoots can be pruned throughout the year. It is advisable to trim the shoots especially when they have reached 5-6 pairs of leaves, to shorten them to 2-3 pairs.

Binding: the metal wire should be applied only on the branches and on the shoots that are quite robust and lignified.

Multiplication: the easiest method is that of multiplication by cuttings.

CHRISTMAS STAR (EUPHORBIA PULCHERRIMA)

Family: euforbiaceae

Description: shrub native to Central America, characterized by a gnarled and rough trunk, vertical branches and light green lobed leaves.

Flowering: in winter reddish inflorescences develop.

Environment and exposure: the poinsettia should be placed in a bright and sunny area, but not exposed to drafts. In winter the recommended temperature is between 15 and 18 degrees Celsius – 59-64 F.

Watering: we recommend watering abundantly throughout the year, keeping the soil constantly humid.

Fertilization: fertilization should be practiced only in the period from March to October, distributing fertilizer once every 2/3 weeks.

Repotting: It is better to repot the Christmas star every year, in the months of March-April, cutting the roots and shortening those that have grown too long.

Soil: the most suitable mixture is made up of 2/5 clay, 2/5 peat and 1/5 sand.

Pruning: the poinsettia needs pruning of branches and shoots only in August.

Binding: given the structure of this plant, tying is not necessary.

Multiplication: methods of multiplication by seed and by cuttings are recommended.

CICAS (CYCAS REVOLUTA)

Family: Cicadaceae

Description: Palm-like plant, native to Japan and characterized by an unbranched stem and elongated dark green leaves erected by a shadow.

Environment and exposure: We recommend keeping it near a well-lit window throughout the year. During the winter the ideal temperature is between 10 and 15 degrees Celsius - 50-59 F..

Watering: Throughout the summer the watering must be abundant and regular; while more moderate doses are recommended during the winter.

Fertilization: For the period from March to September it is good to fertilize once every 2 weeks, with liquid fertilizer. In winter it is preferable to wait 4-5 weeks between one fertilization and another.

Repotting: For Cicas it is sufficient to practice repotting once every 4 or 5 years, cutting the roots and shortening those that are too long.

Soil: A mixture consisting of 1/4 clay, 1/4 peat and 2/4 of sand is recommended, being careful to prepare good drainage.

Pruning: Especially during the spring period it is good to cut the old leaves grown at the base of the stem.

Binding: given the somewhat particular nature of this plant, the binding is superfluous and therefore not recommended.

Multiplication: A good method for obtaining new plants is that of multiplication by seed.

CISSUS ANTARCTICA (CISSUS ANTARCTICA)

Family: Vitaceae

Description: It is an evergreen creeper, originally from Australia. It is characterized by rather rapid growth and a consequent abundance of branches and leaves, which are shaped and have a light green color.

Environment and exposure: Being a robust plant, it can adapt well to different temperatures. It is advisable to keep it, therefore, between 15 and 18 degrees Celsius – 59-64 F., in a fairly illuminated place, throughout the year.

Watering: Accustomed moderate watering, both in summer and in winter.

Fertilization: The period in which it needs more fertilization is from February to October when it can be fertilized once a week. During the winter stasis, it is sufficient to give fertilizer every 5-6 weeks.

Repotting: It is good to repot the still young plants, at least once a year in spring, given their fast growth. For the older ones, it is sufficient once every two years, always in the spring.

Soil: The ideal mixture consists of clay, peat and sand in the same temperatures, both hot and cool, requires proportions.

Pruning: During the vegetative phase it will be carried out frequently. We will have to decrease the number of leaves in the shoots to a number of two and eliminate the leaves that have grown too quickly.

Binding: Can be practiced throughout the year.

Multiplication: Cutting is recommended.

CORK OAK (QUERCUS SUBER)

Family: fagaceae

Description: it is an evergreen and very long-lived tree, native to the Mediterranean areas of Spain, France and Sardinia. It has a wrinkled trunk, silvery green and light green toothed leaves.

Environment and exposure: cork oak can be kept all year round next to a bright window, even if, during the summer it shows that it likes the outdoors and the sun. In winter temperatures between 10 and 15 degrees celsius - 50-59 F. are recommended.

Watering: throughout the summer it is sufficient to keep the soil moist enough; during the winter you can decrease the dose of water, but without ever leaving the soil too dry.

Fertilization: it is necessary to fertilize only in the period between spring and autumn, by administering fertilizer every 2-3 weeks. In winter it is good to stop fertilizing.

Repotting: we recommend practicing repotting once every 2-3 years at the arrival of spring, cutting and shortening the roots.

Soil: to meet the needs of cork oak, the best composition of the soil is made up of soil, peat and sand in equal proportions.

Pruning: branches and shoots can be pruned throughout the year.

Binding: it is advisable to apply the wire only on well-lignified branches and shoots. The best time is summer.

Multiplication: for cork oak, the main methods of obtaining new seedlings are seed multiplication and layering.

CRASSULA ARBORESCENS (CRASSULA ARBORESCENS)

Family: Crassulaceae

Description: It is a tree from southern Africa with thick and fleshy green leaves. The trunk is dark but bright. It can reach a maximum height of 2-3 yards.

Environment and exposure: It can be at home next to a Juminosa window, but not in the sun, or outside from May to September in a shady place. The ideal temperature for winter is between 10 and 15 degrees Celsius – 50-59 F..

Watering: Being a plant that resists dry even for a month, it is best not to water it excessively. In summer, therefore, the watering will be moderate, and the interval times in winter will further expand.

Fertilization: In the period from May to September the liquid fertilizer will be supplied every month, while during the summer stasis the administration will stop.

Repotting: Once a year, cutting and shortening the roots. After repotting it is good not to water for 2 weeks.

Soil: The ideal soil is made up of 1/5 clay, peat for 2/5 and sand for 2/5.

Pruning: The branches can be pruned throughout the spring-summer period. The shoots must be sprouted when groups of leaves have formed, so as to leave only two or three pairs of leaves.

Binding: Can be done on branches and shoots throughout the year.

Multiplication: Excellent results can be obtained with the cutting method. The most suitable methods for obtaining new plants

CRYPTOMERIA (CRYPTOMERIA JAPONICA)

Family: taxodiaceae

Description: large conifer native to the forests of central Japan and southern China. It is characterized by a dark red bark, hanging branches and spiral-shaped persistent leaves.

Environment and exposure: it is important to always keep it in a bright, dark place, without letting the sun hit it. For the winter the ideal temperature is between 8 and 15 degrees Celsius - 46-59 F.

Watering: throughout the year it is good to water abundantly and regularly, spraying the leaves two or three times a week.

Fertilization: fertilization must be applied for the entire period from March to October, with liquid fertilizer distributed once every 3-4 weeks.

Repotting: we recommend repotting Cryptomeria once every 3 or 4 years, in the months of March and April, shortening overgrown roots.

Soil: the most suitable mixture for the best development of the plant consists of 2/5 of clay, 1/5 of peat and 2/5 of sand.

Pruning: in spring it is recommended to prune the branches. The shoots, on the other hand, are topped both in spring and autumn, shortening them by 2/3.

Binding: for Cryptomeria March is the best time to tie branches and shoots, provided they are well lignified.

Multiplication: the most suitable methods for obtaining new plants are those by seed and by cutting.

DAISY (CHRYSANTHEMUM)

Family: composite

Description: it is a plant native to China, with numerous erect stems that can reach a height of 27-32 inch. The leaves are green and elongated.

Flowering: in the period between May and August, 2 inch diameter flowers with yellow central eye and white, yellow or purple petals appear on the lignified branches according to the various species.

Environment and exposure: all year round it can be kept in a very bright and sunny place. In summer it is recommended to stay outdoors, in the sun. The temperature at which it is good to keep it during the winter is around 15-18 degrees Celsius – 59-64 F.

Watering: the water should be given abundantly and regularly throughout, but especially in the summer.

Fertilization: the fertilizer must be supplied throughout the year except in the flowering period. From spring to autumn, a 2-3 weeks dose is recommended.

Repotting: we recommend repotting once every 2-3 years, when spring arrives, cutting and sprouting overgrown roots.

Soil: the ideal soil for growing daisy is made up of 2/5 clay, 2/5 peat and 1/5 sand.

Pruning: the most suitable period for pruning branches and shoots is at the end of flowering. Anticipating the operational risks that flowering will not take place.

Binding: slightly lignified branches and shoots can be tied, even if the application of the wire is often not necessary.

Multiplication: multiplication methods by seed are recommended every in winter one dose every 4-5 weeks. by cuttings.

DWARF ORANGE (FORTUNELLA HINDSII)

Family: Rutaceae

Description: It is a subtropical tree from eastern Asia and the Mediterranean area, characterized by small leaves and fruits.

Flowering: Dwarf orange will begin to give small and fragrant flowers only in adulthood.

Environment and exposure: All year round it can be kept indoors, in a bright and well-ventilated place. For the period from May to September, it can be placed outdoors in the sun or dim light. During the winter keep the temperature between 5 and 10 degrees Celsius - 41-50 F..

Watering: In summer it will be practiced often and in abundance. In winter it will be sufficient to water only when it is dry.

Fertilization: It is better to fertilize every 2 weeks in the summer. Increase the period in autumn and spring, until it stops in winter.

Repotting: This should be practiced every 2-3 years, at the beginning of spring, popping up and cutting the roots.

Soil: Good soil is made up of clay, peat and sand in equal proportions.

Pruning: Care must be taken to prune the branches because they do not grow back easily. The shoots must be cut to leave groups of 2-3 leaves.

Binding: Can be practiced on already robust and lignified branches and shoots.

Multiplication: The seed method is recommended

ERETHIA BUXIFOLIA (CARMONA MICROPHYLLA)

Family: boraginaceae

Description: it is an evergreen shrub from the tropical areas of southern China and south-east Asia. The trunk is of a silvery green color, and develops dark green oval leaves. In the period following flowering, the berries appear to change from green to red.

Flowering: from spring to summer white flowers bloom.

Environment and exposure: being a tropical plant, it is well suited to the internal temperatures of the house (15-24 degrees Celsius – 59-75 F.). It is always best to keep it in a bright place and not expose it to the sun. In the period between May and September it can be outside.

Watering: it is advisable to water abundantly throughout the year.

Fertilization: during the vegetative phase of greater intensity, between March and September, it is better to fertilize every 2 weeks with liquid fertilizer. In winter it is good to limit fertilization to once every 4 weeks.

Repotting: to be carried out always in spring and every two years, cutting and shortening the roots.

Soil: the recommended mixture is 2/5 of soil for bonsai, 2/5 of peat or May and September can be outside. "year. peat and 1/5

Pruning: the branches can always be pruned, while in the shoots the leaves will be decreased from groups of 6 or more to groups of 2 or 3.

Binding: you can apply the metal wire throughout the whole Sprouts can be tied only if they are strong and lignified enough

Multiplication: the method by cutting or by seed is recommended.

EUFORBIA (EUPHORBIA BALSAMIFERA)

Family: euphorbiaceae

Description: it is a cactaceous shrub native to West Africa which, like all plants in the family, has white latex inside, which comes out of any wounds on the trunk.

Environment and exposure: it can be at home next to a window all year round, in winter the temperature must remain between 10 and 15 degrees Celsius – 50-59 F. You can take it outside in summer without worrying too much about the sun, given its structure.

Watering: for the summer period it is sufficient to water once a week. During the winter, however, once every 2 weeks. When the plant begins to lose the leaves, you have to stop until they are reappeared.

Fertilization: to be practiced only in the period between May and September once a month.

Repotting: once a year in spring, shortening the roots. After repotting it is good not to water for 2 weeks.

Soil: the most suitable mixture consists of 1/5 of clay, 2/5 of sand and 2/5 of peat.

Pruning: it is better to prune branches and shoots between spring and summer. When latex comes out, it is better to dry it quickly, to avoid sticking.

Binding: it is not very suitable for this type of plant.

Multiplication: multiplications by cutting and by seeds are recommended.

FERN (GREVILLEA ROBUST)

Family: protaceae

Description: The tree fern is a tree with large flowers and broad, pinnate leaves, native to Western Australia.

Environment and exposure: it can be placed in front of a bright window, but not in the sun. In winter it is advisable to keep the temperature between 12 and 15 degrees Celsius – 53-59 F.

Watering: throughout the year it is best to water continuously to keep the soil always moist.

Fertilization: it must be fertilized only in the vegetative period and in summer, preferably using liquid fertilizer, once every two weeks.

Repotting: repotting must be practiced annually during the spring, sprouting and cutting the roots.

Soil: The most suitable mixture for tree fern is made up of 2/5 clay, 1/5 peat and 2/5 sand.

Pruning: the branches can be pruned throughout the year. It is good to trim the shoots, removing excess leaves and those that have become too large.

Binding: branches and shoots as long as they are strong enough for the metal wire.

Multiplication: multiplication by cutting or seed is recommended.

FICUS (RETUSA GINSENG)

Family: Moracee

Description: They can be found on every continent in the tropic regions.

Placement: The ficus is an indoor tree that does not endure frosty conditions. It can be kept outside in the summer as long as temperatures are above 60°F (15°C). It requires a lot of light, preferably full sunlight, so be sure not to place it in a shady location. The temperature should be kept relatively constant. Figs can endure low humidity due to their thick, waxy leaves, but they prefer higher humidity and need extremely high humidity to develop aerial roots.

Watering : The Ficus should be watered normally, which means it should be given water generously whenever the soil gets slightly dry. The Bonsai Ficus prefers room temperature soft water and it can tolerate occasional over, or underwatering. We advise daily misting to maintain humidity, but too much misting can create fungal problems. The warmer the placement of the fig during winter the more water it needs. If it's kept in a cooler place it only needs to be kept slightly moist.

Fertilizing : Fertilize every two weeks during summer, and every four weeks during winter if the growth doesn't stop. Liquid fertilizer can be used as well as organic fertilizer pellets.

Pruning: Regular pruning is necessary to retain the tree's shape. Prune back to 2 leaves after 6-8 leaves have grown. Leaf pruning (defoliation) can be used to reduce leaf size, as some Ficus Bonsai species normally grow large leaves. If a considerable thickening of the trunk is desired, the Ficus can be left to grow freely for one or two years. The strong cuts that are necessary afterward don't affect the Ficus' health and new shoots will grow from old wood. Larger wounds should be covered with cut paste

Wiring: Wiring and bending thin to medium Ficus branches is easy due to their flexibility, but you should check the wires regularly as they can cut into the bark very quickly. Strong branches should be shaped with guy-wires because they can be left on the tree for a much longer period.

Repotting: During the spring, every other year, using a basic Bonsai soil mixture. Ficus tolerates root-pruning very well.

Propagation: Cuttings can be planted at any time of the year, but they have the highest success rate during mid-summer growth. Air-layering will work best during spring, in April through May. In most cases, springtime is the best time for planting Ficus seeds.

Pests / diseases: Species are quite resistant against pests, but they are still susceptible to several issues depending on their location, and time of year, especially in the winter. Dry air and a lack of light weakens the Bonsai Ficus and often result in leaf drop. In poor conditions like these, they are sometimes infested with scale or spider mites. Placing customary insecticide sticks into the soil or spraying insecticide/miticide will get rid of the pests, but a weakened Ficus tree's living conditions must be improved. Using plant lamps 12 to 14 hours a day, and frequently misting the leaves will help in the recovery process.

FUCHSIA (FUCHSIA FULGENS HYBRIDA)

Family: onagraceae

Description: it is a plant native to Central and South America, characterized by soft dark green leaves and reddish flowers.

Environment and exposure: throughout the year it can be next to a bright window. In summer it can also be placed outdoors, in an area away from direct sunlight. For the winter it is good to keep a temperature around 10 degrees Celsius - 50 F., in a bright place.

Watering: in summer it can be watered abundantly to guarantee constant soil moisture. In winter it is better to decrease the amount of water, leaving the soil a little drier.

Fertilization: for the period from March to September, it can be fertilized once every 2 weeks. In winter it is best to reduce fertilization to once every 4 weeks.

Repotting: every year, or every two years, at the arrival of spring it is good to repot, cutting the roots and trimming the shoots.

Soil: the most suitable soil consists of equal proportions of sand, clay and pruning: the branches can always be pruned, the shoots only once the flowering is finished.

Binding: Fuchsia is not suitable for binding with metal wire, due to the rather fragile structure.

Multiplication: cutting is possible with excellent results.

GARDENIA (GARDENIA JASMINOIDES)

Family: rubiaceae

Description: Gardenia is an evergreen shrub, native to East Asia. It has very abundant branches and dark green leathery leaves.

Flowering: usually during the winter white flowers with an intense fragrance appears.

Environment and exposure: throughout the year it can be placed in a bright and ventilated place, but not exposed to direct sun. In winter we recommend a temperature between 12 and 18 degrees Celsius – 53-65 F.

Watering: in summer it will be practiced in sufficient quantity to keep the soil starch. In winter it is important not to leave the soil dry for too long.

Fertilization: it is good to fertilize with liquid fertilizer, and exclusively in the period from March to September with liquid fertilizer.

Repotting: you can repot once every year, or every two years, sprouting the roots.

Soil: a mixture of 1/6 clay, 3/6 peat and 2/6 sand will be prepared.

Binding: the branches and shoots can be tied as long as they are sufficiently lignified.

Pruning: the branches can always be pruned, while shoots are topped only after flowering.

Multiplication: Multiplication by cutting is recommended.

GINCO (GINKGO BILOBA)

Family: gincoaceae

Description: tree native to eastern China, characterized by thin bark, abundant branches and petiolate leaves similar to a fan.

Environment and exposure: it must be kept near a bright window throughout the year, avoiding exposing it to direct sun. For the winter the best temperature varies between 10 and 15 degrees Celsius – 50-59 F.

Watering: for the summer period it is advisable to water normally and regularly. In winter it is best to provide water only once a day.

Fertilization: for everything you need to fertilize once every 3-4 weeks. In winter it is better to suspend the period between March and April,

Repotting: it is recommended once every year, cutting

Soil: the most suitable mixture for this plant is made up of 1/5 of clay, 2/5 of peat and 2/5 of sand.

Pruning: branches should be pruned in mid-spring during the repotting period. It is recommended to eliminate the shoots in early spring.

Binding: the most suitable period for binding is June on well-lignified branches and shoots.

Multiplication: the best way to get new plants is to multiply by seed.

JAPANESE MAPLE (ACER PALMATUM)

Family: Sapindaceae

Description: Otherwise known as Acer palmatum, is originally from Far East. It owes its botanical name to the hand-shaped leaves with five pointed lobes. Palma is Latin for palm, as in the palm of your hand. Younger trees usually have green or reddish bark that turns light grey or grayish brown as it ages.

Environment and exposure: Environment and exposure: the tree do really well in sunny and airy location, but when temperatures rise to 85 °F (30 °C) or above, it should be placed somewhere with indirect sunlight to prevent damaging the leaves. It is frost hardy, even when trained as a Bonsai, but when temperatures drop below 15 °F (-10 °C), it should be protected.

Watering: Must be watered daily during the growing season. During the hotter days in the growing season, it's sometimes necessary to water your tree several times, if the soil is well-drained and the tree is healthy and vigorous. Avoid watering with calcareous water as prefer a neutral or slightly acid pH-value.

Flowering: Small, hanging clusters of bright red flowers appear in spring before the leaves. Two red maple trees may look different from each other during the flowering period. Red Maples can produce all male flowers, all female flowers, or some of both.

Fertilizing: Fertilizing: Solid, organic fertilizers contain all the required micronutrients, and they take effect slowly and gently. If you'd like a stronger growth on young plants, you can combine your regular dosage with a liquid fertilizer once a week. Avoid fertilizers with a high nitrogen concentration to avoid unnecessarily large leaves and internodes.

Repotting: The Bonsai should be repotted every two years. It has strong roots that grow quickly and usually fill the pot in a short time, so be sure to prune the roots efficiently.

Pruning: Strong branches should be pruned in autumn or summer, when callus growth is quick, to prevent excessive bleeding. When pruning thick branches we advise using a cut paste product to prevent fungal diseases that can enter through pruning wounds. New growth should be pruned back to one or two pairs of leaves. Mature Bonsai with a delicate ramification can be pinched in order to keep the twigs thin. After the first leaf pair has unfolded, remove the soft little tip of the shoot between them to prevent the twigs from thickening. Leaf pruning is the removal of all leaves during the growing season to encourage a second and often finer flush of growth. It should not be done every year because it puts quite a bit of stress on the tree. When pruning, remove all the leaves, but make sure to leave the leaf-stems intact. Partial leaf pruning is a more gentle and less stressful pruning method, so it can be done every year. Remove the largest leaves, closely spaced leaves, or the leaves in the strongest areas of the tree.

Multiplication: The Japanese maple can easily be propagated by planting seeds, cuttings, or air layering in the summer.

Soil: Use a well-drained soil mixture with Pumice and lava rock.

Japanese maples are fairly adaptive, but prefer moist, well-drained, slightly acidic soils that contain organic matter. If you live in an area with heavy clay soil, planting them slightly elevated is beneficial; this will help guard against root rot and disease. Chlorosis (yellowing of leaves due to lack of chlorophyll) may occur in high-pH soils.

JUBUTICABA (MYRCIARIA CAULIFLORA)

Family: myrtaceae

Description: it is a tropical shrub from Brazil and South America. The bark is spotted and the branches, very numerous, have oval and elongated light green leaves.

Flowering: in the branches develop white inflorescences composed of small flowers, on which dark berries are formed. However, the plant rarely blooms in cold areas, with a climate so different from the original one.

Environment and exposure: the Jubuticaba can be kept near a bright window throughout the year, the important thing is not to subject it directly to sunlight. In winter it should be kept at a temperature of 18-20 degrees Celsius – 64-68 F.

Watering: summer it is recommended to water often and in good quantities. In winter it is good to reduce the doses of water to keep the soil at constant humidity.

Fertilization: in the period from spring to autumn it is good to fertilize every 2 weeks. As winter approaches, fertilization should be limited to once every 4-5 weeks.

Repotting: to be practiced every two years during the spring, cutting and sprouting the roots.

Soil: the ideal mixture for Jubuticaba is made up of 1/5 of clay, 2/5 of sand and 2/5 of peat.

Pruning: it is essential to trim the shoots so as to have only one or two pairs of leaves. Branches can always be cut.

Binding: wire binding is recommended only on those well-lignified branches and shoots.

Multiplication: the most suitable method for this type of plant is multiplication by seed.

LANTANA (LANTANA CAMARA)

Family: verbenaceae

Description: Lantana is a tropical evergreen shrub with dark green oval leaves, the trunk is light gray, tending to brown.

Flowering: during the summer it produces flowers with shades ranging from yellow to red.

Environment and exposure: just place the Lantana in a bright place and during the summer it is recommended to take it outside without exposing it to the intense sun for too long. For the winter it is good to maintain a temperature between 15 and 20 degrees Celsius - 59-68 F.

Watering: in summer it is advisable to water frequently, to keep the soil moist. In winter it is better to decrease the doses.

Fertilization: for the period from March to September it is recommended to administer liquid fertilizer every 2 weeks. In winter, however, it is sufficient to fertilize every 4-5 weeks 20 degrees Celsius – 68 F.

Repotting: it should be practiced once every two years, at the arrival of spring, by shortening and cutting the roots.

Soil: we recommend a mixture composed of 1/5 of clay, 2/5 of sand 2/5 of peat.

Pruning: the branches can be pruned throughout the year, while shoots are topped only after flowering.

Binding: it is possible to apply the metal wire, an operation to be carried out delicately, due to the fragile structure of the branches of the lantana.

Multiplication: methods by cutting or by seed are particularly suitable.

LEBANON CEDAR (CEDRUS LIBANI)

Family: Pinaceae

Description: It is an evergreen tree, native to Mediterranean areas and southern Asia. It has horizontal branches and needle-like leaves gathered in bundles. It produces ovoid and woody fruits.

Environment and exposure: We recommend keeping the plant in a very bright and ventilated area, possibly near a window. It can be taken outside for the summer period. In winter it is good to maintain a temperature of 10-15 degrees Celsius – 50-59 F..

Watering: It is good to water abundantly and regularly throughout the year, keeping in soil.

Fertilization: It is necessary to fertilize only in the period from March to October, distributing fertilizer once every 2-3 weeks.

Repotting: The best time to repot is once every two years, in the period of the spring preceding the development of new shoots. It is good to cut and shorten the roots.

Soil: The most suitable mixture for good development of the plant consists of 2/5 of clay, 2/5 of peat, and 1/5 of sand.

Pruning: We recommend pruning the branches in early spring. The shoots must be pruned during the summer by shearing them so as to leave only 2-3 needle whorls.

Binding: Cedar of Lebanon can be tied at any time of the year, paying attention to the strength of the branches and shoots.

Multiplication: The most suitable method for multiplying Cedar is by seed.

LEMON (CITRUS LIMON) –

Family: rutaceae

Description: tree from western Asia, characterized by the dark brown trunk, slightly rough, pointed oval leaves always green.

Flowering: in spring, white flowers appear isolated or in pairs. The fruit is oval and smooth, green in development and yellow when ripe.

Environment and exposure: all year round it can be kept next to a bright window. In summer it is recommended to take it outside, placing it even in full sun. For winter, the ideal temperature is between 5 and 10 degrees Celsius – 50-59 F.

Watering: between spring and summer the watering will be regular, to be done on dry soil. In winter it is sufficient to water once a day.

Fertilization: between spring and autumn it is recommended to fertilize once every 2-3 weeks, stopping during flowering and fruiting. In winter it is sufficient to fertilize every 4-5 weeks.

Repotting: repotting should be practiced once every 3-4 years, at the arrival of spring, by cutting and sprouting too long roots.

Soil: the most suitable mixture consists of 2/4 of clay, 1/4 of peat and 1/4 of sand.

Pruning: the branches can be pruned from April to September, while the shoots are topped with 2-3 pairs of leaves when they have reached 5-6 pairs.

Binding: spring is the best time to bind the lemon, using paper-covered metal wire on sturdy branches and shoots.

Multiplication: especially the cutting method to be practiced in spring is recommended.

MAGNOLIA (MAGNOLIA STELLATA)

Family: magnoliaceae

Description: shrub native to Europe, Asia and North America, characterized by abundant branches and large, oval leaves.

Flowering: in the late spring period, very fragrant flowers sprout from the petals of a pure white.

Environment and exposure: we recommend keeping the plant in front of a window, also exposing it to direct sunlight. For the summer period, it can also be placed outdoors. In winter it is sufficient to keep it at a temperature of 12-18 degrees Celsius - 53-64 F.

Watering: Magnolia should be watered in moderation throughout the year; therefore, it is advisable to distribute water in sufficient quantities, and that the soil remains dry too long.

Fertilization: the fertilizer must be administered exclusively in the fertilizing period after flowering and until the end of October. It is good to use liquid fertilizer once every 2-3 weeks.

Repotting: it should be practiced once a year, at the arrival of spring, cutting the roots and sprouting those that have grown excessively.

Soil: the most suitable mixture consists of 2/5 of clay, 2/5 of peat and 1/5 of sand.

Pruning: the branches should be pruned in the spring, when the first ones appear. It is recommended to cut the shoots at the end of flowering, Pruning If On 4-5 pairs of leaves to 1-2 couples.

Binding: the best period for the application of the metal wire is in the summer, on already lignified and sufficiently robust branches and shoots.

Multiplication: good results are obtained by multiplication by seed and by cutting.

MARJORAM (MAJORANA HORTENSIS)

Family: labiateae

Description: it is a fragrant and aromatic plant, native to Asia and boreal Africa, it has an erect trunk and oval, fragrant, green-white leaves.

Flowering: in the period immediately, preceding summer produces small flowers, white or pink.

Environment and exposure: it can be kept all year round in a ventilated and bright area. During the summer it adapts very well to being placed outside, in a sunny place, while in winter it prefers temperatures between 5 and 12.

Watering: for the summer it is advisable to water abundantly, especially if it does very hot. In winter it is better to reduce the amount of water, limiting to supplying it only when the soil is dry.

Fertilization: fertilization should be practiced especially in the spring and autumn, by administering fertilizer once every 2 weeks.

Repotting: repotting should be done once every 3-4 years, with the arrival of spring, cutting and sprouting the roots slightly.

Soil: the ideal mixture for marjoram is made up of 2/5 clay, 2/5 peat and 1/5 sand, all grades.

Pruning: It is recommended to cut the shoots by decreasing the number of leaves from 5-6 pairs to 2-3. The branches should be pruned especially in the autumn period.

Binding: given the structure of the marjoram, the application of the metal wire is of little use.

Multiplication: the two most recommended methods for obtaining new bonsai plants are by cutting and by seed.

MULBERRY-TREE (MORUS ALBA)

Family: moraceae

Description: it is a tree characteristic of the areas of Europe and southern Asia. It has a wrinkled trunk, gray-brown color and smooth and elongated gray-green branches. The leaves, used for the breeding of the silkworm, are wide, serrated and smooth,

Environment and exposure: The Mulberry can be kept next to a window, in a bright and ventilated area. In the summer it can be taken outside, in a sunny area, while avoiding the afternoon sun. In winter the best temperature is between 10 and 15 degrees Celsius – 50-59 F.

Watering: for the period from March to October, water regularly and in abundance, to keep the soil moist. In winter, the distribution of water can be limited, waiting for the soil to be dry.

Fertilization: Mulberry must be fertilized exclusively in the spring and summer period, by administering fertilizer once every 2-3 weeks.

Repotting: repotting should be practiced once every year in late spring.

Soil: the most suitable mixture for mulberry is made up of 2/5 clay, 2/5 peat and 1/5 sand. of a light green color. so, the best time for pruning the branches in spring. It is recommended to prune the shoots when they have reached a length of 0.5 inch.

Binding: binding is preferably done in spring and summer, on lignified branches and shoots, with metal wire covered with paper.

Multiplication: the method that obtains the best results in mulberry multiplication is by seed.

MURRAYA PANICULATA (MURRAYA PANICULATA)

Family: rutaceae

Description: small tropical tree from southern China and India. It has a light brown trunk and small, light green leaves.

Flowering: in the final period of summer, between August and September, the murraya produces very fragrant white bell-shaped flowers, and subsequently, at the end of October, elongated reddish berries.

Environment and exposure: it is possible to leave the murraya all year round in a bright and airy area, while not leaving it in the direct rays of the sun. In winter it is best to keep it at temperatures between 15 and 20 degrees Celsius – 59-68 F.

Watering: it is advisable to water often, to keep the soil moist throughout the year.

Fertilization: throughout the vegetative period, until autumn, it is advisable to administer liquid fertilizer every two weeks. In winter, however, it is sufficient to fertilize once every 4-5 weeks.

Repotting: the murraya must be repotted once every two years during the spring, sprouting and cutting the roots.

Soil: it is advisable to prepare a mixture of 2/5 of clay, 2/5 of peat and 1/5 of sand.

Pruning: the branches can be pruned throughout the year, on the contrary, it is good to tick the shoots in pairs of 2 leaves, only when they have reached groups of 4 or 5 leaves.

Binding: it can be practiced throughout the year both on the trunk and on the branches.

Multiplication: the ideal for Murraya is to use the seeds of the berries, planting them in rather hot soil.

MYRTLE CRESPO (LAGERSTROEMIA INDICA)

Family: lytraceae

Description: subtropical shrub from China and Japan, characterized by the brown trunk, tending to pink and oval deciduous leaves of light green color.

Flowering: in summer, white, pink, or purple flowers bloom on the shoots that have reached one year of life.

Environment and exposure: throughout the year it must be arranged indoors, in a bright and airy area. For the summer it can also be taken outside, and also exposed to the sun, provided that it is done in moderation. In winter it is good to keep it at a temperature of 5-10 degrees Celsius – 41-50 F.

Watering: in summer it is good to water abundantly especially when it is very hot. In winter it is recommended to decrease the amount of water, while keeping the soil slightly moistened.

Fertilization: it is recommended only in the period between March and September, with liquid fertilizer, once every two weeks.

Repotting: it is good to repot once every two years at the beginning of the spring, by trimming and cutting the roots.

Soil: the right mixture is made up of 1/4 clay, 2/4 peat and 1/4 sand.

Pruning: branches can always be pruned. The shoots, on the other hand, must be trimmed until they leave one or two pairs of leaves. However, those shoots on which you want to grow flowers will not be topped.

Binding: aluminum wire can be applied throughout the year except during the flowering period and on non-lignified branches and shoots.

Multiplication: seed and cutting methods are recommended.

NEEDLE JUNIPER (JUNIPERUS RIGIDA)

Family: cupressaceae

Description: evergreen shrub, characteristic of the mountainous areas of Mediterranean and central Europe. It has a thin bark, with needle-like and pungent leaves of a blue-green color.

Flowering: during late spring it produces yellow, male, and greenish, female flowers. Subsequently, bacchiform fruits develop.

Environment and exposure: it is advisable to keep the plant in a very bright place and also in the sun, provided that it is not too direct and intense. For the summer it can be taken outdoors, while in winter it prefers temperatures between 8 and 14 degrees Celsius - 46-57 F.

Watering: for the summer it is good to water regularly, so as to keep the soil moist. In winter it is enough to prevent the soil from drying out the ovals, too.

Fertilization: in the period from March until October it is possible to fertilize once every 2-3 weeks, stopping during flowering. In winter it is sufficient once every 4-5 weeks.

Repotting: it is recommended to practice repotting every 2 years, in the periods of March-April, cutting and sprouting the roots.

Soil: the ideal mixture consists of clay, peat and sand in the following proportions: 2/5, 1/5 and 2/5.

Pruning: the branches can be pruned throughout the year. The shoots, however, only from summer to autumn, shortening them by 2/3 when they have reached 1 inch.

Binding: branches and shoots can be tied with wire preferably during March-April and September-October and only if sufficiently robust and lignified.

Multiplication: to obtain a new plant we especially recommend the seed method.

OAK (QUERCUS)

Family: Fagaceae

Description: most are deciduous but some are evergreen, they produce characteristic fruits, acorns. There are several hundred oak species which grow in Europe, North Africa, Southwest Asia, Central and North America.

Flowering: It has male and female flowers on the same tree. Male flowers are on catkins and hang down, female flowers are small and red and located on short stalks called peduncles. Catkins release pollen in April and May and the red female flowers develop into acorns by autumn.

Environment and exposure: Oak trees prefer an airy place in full sun during the growing season. The European Oak, the White Oak and other northern oak species are frost hardy when they are growing in the ground, but they need winter protection when they are planted in containers.

Watering: Water the oak thoroughly when the soil gets dry, but avoid constant soil wetness. Water less in winter but never let the rootball dry out completely.

Fertilization: Apply solid organic fertilizer once a month or use a liquid fertilizer every week during the growing season. Don't feed with very high nitrogen which would cause large leaves, long internodes and increased susceptibility to insects and mildew.

Repotting: Young oaks should be repotted every two years, older ones every three to five years in spring before the buds open. Don't cut off more than one third of the roots.

Soil: Only when the soil looks light brown and feels damp will your bonsai require more water. Water thoroughly all over the soil until the water drains through the drainage holes in the bottom of the pot. Never let your bonsai dry out and avoid keeping it constantly wet. The soil should go from wet to damp between watering. Remember the hotter the position the more water your bonsai will use. If the soil surface becomes hard during hot weather simply submerge your bonsai in water, to cover the soil surface, for about ten minutes.

Pruning: Hard pruning is done in early spring before the buds open. Strong terminal buds can also be removed then. New shoots are cut back leaving two leaves. Don't defoliate oaks completely because it would weaken them too much, but you can remove the largest leaves now and then. Trim the upper parts of the crown attentively because they grow stronger than the lower branches.

Binding: When oaks are wired be careful to remove the wire before it bites into the bark. Wire marks will be visible for a very long time. Guy wires can be a good choice instead.

Multiplication: Oaks are easily propagated from seed. Cuttings and air-layers don't root in most cases.

OLIVE (OLEA EUROPEA)

Family: oleaceae

Description: tree native to the Mediterranean coast, characterized by wrinkled trunk and branches and a silver-gray-green color. The leaves are elongated and a silvery green color.

Flowering: from the end of April to that of June dark flowers begin to appear and around mid-July also black fruits grow.

Environment and exposure: throughout the year it can be kept in front of a well-lit and even sunny window. In the summer, until the beginning of autumn, it can be kept outdoors in a semi-shady or sunny place. In winter, the ideal temperature is between 8 and 15 degrees Celsius - 46-59 F..

Watering: the method of watering is constant throughout the year and consists of providing water only once the soil has become dry.

Fertilization: it is good to practice fertilizing only in the period from spring to the end of summer, using liquid fertilizer once every 3 weeks. In winter, the administration is stopped.

Repotting: we recommend repotting the olive tree once every two years at the arrival of spring, cutting and shortening the roots.

Soil: the mixture a more for the Olive is based on clay for 2/5, for the remaining 2/5. 1/5 peat and suitable sand

Pruning: branches can always be pruned. The shoots are topped to decrease the number of leaves to two or three pairs. In any case, be careful because the olive tree does not throw new jets very easily.

Binding: only branches and shoots that have already achieved good strength should be tied.

Multiplication: The best ways to get new plants are by multiplication by cuttings and by seed.

OSMANTO (OSMANTHUS ILICIFOLIUS)

Family: oleaceae

Description: evergreen shrub from south-eastern Asia. It has thick branches and persistent, serrated leaves of bright green color.

Flowering: develops small yellowish-white flowers and later ovoid black-bluish fruits.

Environment and exposure: it is always important to place the plant in a bright and ventilated place. In summer it can be taken outdoors in the shade and the sun, if not too strong. In winter it should be kept at cool temperatures between 3 and 10 degrees Celsius – 37-50 F.

Watering: for the entire period between February and November it is necessary to water abundantly. During the winter, however, it is sufficient to wait for the soil to dry completely, before watering again.

Fertilization: it can be fertilized in the period from March to October, however it is good to suspend the administration of fertilizer during flowering.

Repotting: it is necessary to repot the plant once every 2-3 years, shortening and cutting the roots.

Soil: the ideal mixture for Osmanthus is made up of 2/5 clay, 2/5 peat and 1/5 sand.

Pruning: it is possible to prune the branches at any time of the year, while the shoots will be clipped to 2-3 pairs of leaves, when they have reached 5-6 pairs.

Binding: it is recommended to apply the wire in the spring and autumn.

Multiplication: multiplication by seed is recommended, even if we remember that it is possible to obtain good results with that by air layering.

PEACH (PRUNUS PERSICA) –

Family: rosaceae

Description: it is a fruit tree, originally from northern China. characterized by the dark gray trunk, large and smooth branches and elongated and serrated leaves of green color in the upper surface and green-gray in the lower one.

Flowering: in spring, on the branches of a year, solitary pink, white or reddish flowers sprout. Later the homonymous fruits developed.

Environment and exposure: it is recommended to place the plant next to a window in a ventilated and bright area. During the summer it can also be taken outside, in twilight or a sunny place. In winter it is good to keep the temperature between 12 and 18 degrees Celsius – 56 – 64 F.

Watering: throughout the year it is advisable to water abundantly and regularly, avoiding that the soil remains dry for too long.

Fertilization: the right time for fertilization goes from March to October, distributing fertilizer once every 2-3 weeks.

Repotting: it is advisable to practice repotting once a year, in spring, or in September, sprouting overgrown roots.

Soil: the most suitable soil for Peach is a mixture consisting of 2/5 clay, 2/5 peat and 1/5 sand.

Pruning: the branches can be pruned throughout the year, but especially after the flowering period is recommended. The shoots, however, must be trimmed in early summer.

Binding: the application of the metal wire should be practiced preferably during the month of June on lignified branches and shoots,

Multiplication: to obtain new bonsai plants, the methods by cutting and by seed are recommended.

PINE (PINO SILVESTRIS)

Family: pinaceae

Description: evergreen conifer characteristic of central-northern areas of Europe. It has an oval crown, with reddish young branches and gray adult branches. The leaves are spiral twisted and green-blue in color.

Environment and exposure: it is advisable to keep the plant in a bright and ventilated area. For the summer period, it can be left outdoors, even in the sun. In winter temperature between 8 and 15 degrees celsius - 46-59 F.is required.

Watering: the Pine needs a lot of water, therefore it is necessary to water abundantly and regularly throughout the year.

Fertilization: between the months of January and October it is advisable to distribute the fertilizer once every 2-3 weeks. In winter, however, it is sufficient to allow 4-5 weeks to pass between one distribution and another.

Repotting: repotting should be practiced once every two years, in the period just before the appearance of the sprouts or in the months of September and October.

Soil: the most suitable mixture for growing pine is made up of 1/4 clay, 2/4 peat and 1/4 sand.

Pruning: the branches should preferably be pruned in the spring and autumn months, the shoots, however, during the summer, removing them completely.

Binding: the best time to apply the metal wire is from September to January.

Multiplication: multiplication by seed and by cutting are, in general, the most used methods. you.

PISTACHIO (PISTACIA CHINENSIS)

Family: anacardiaceae

Description: it is a tree native to Syria and later spread in the Mediterranean area and in southern Asia. It has a grayish trunk and abundant branches. The leaves are dense, pointed and light green in color. During the late summer period, it produces the homonymous fruits.

Environment and exposure: we recommend keeping the Pistachio inside, next to a window, in a bright and airy area. The exterior is recommended only in the summer and in an area not directly lit by the sun. During the winter it is good to keep it at a temperature between 15 and 20 degrees Celsius – 59-68 F.

Watering: both in summer and in winter it is advisable to water with a certain regularity, so as not to let the soil dry completely. Sometimes it may be necessary to spray.

Fertilization: during the period between spring and autumn it is recommended to fertilize once every 2 weeks, with liquid fertilizer. In winter, the administration of fertilizer will be reduced to once every 5-6 weeks.

Repotting: repotting should be carried out once every 2-3 years, during the spring period, by cutting and sprouting overgrown roots.

Soil: the recommended mixture for Pistachio is made up of 2/5 peat, 2/5 clay and 1/5 sand.

Pruning: the branches can be pruned throughout the year. The shoots are to be pruned when they have reached 5-6 pairs of leaves, reducing them to 2-3 pairs.

Binding: the metal wire can be applied throughout the year, paying attention to the branches and shoots not yet lignified.

Multiplication: the method most suited to Pistachio is constituted by multiplication by seed.

PITTOSPORUM (PITTOSPORUM TOBIRA)

Family: Pittosporaceae

Description: Pittosporum are evergreen shrubs or small trees. They have thick, glossy, dark grey, leathery leaves. Flowers are rather small and creamy white in colour. At maturity they produce a leathery fruit called a capsule. They are quite tolerant of salt sprays and strong winds common along coastal regions.

Environment and exposure: They will tolerate full sun and will thrive in shaded areas. Will tolerate temperatures of twenty degrees F or less without noticeable injury.

Watering: Adequate water to keep from drying out. Feeding: General purpose fertilizer.

Pruning and wiring: The tree has no particular natural form making it a candidate for informal upright.

Propagation: May be propagated by tip cuttings. Seeds are difficult to obtain and viability is usually poor. Grafting is useful.

Repotting: The tree needs annual repotting and may be severely root pruned. The soil should be well draining.

PLANTING WILLOW (SALIX BABYLONICA)

Family: salicaceae

Description: tree with thick foliage, native to the Far East, characterized by flexible and hanging branches with elongated and gray-green leaves.

Environment and exposure: the ideal place is a bright and ventilated area. During the summer it can be taken outdoors, trying to avoid the afternoon sun. In winter the recommended temperature varies between 12 and 18 degrees Celsius – 56-64 F..

Watering: it is important to always keep the soil moist, even in winter, therefore it will be necessary to water abundantly.

Fertilization: fertilization must be practiced in the months between March and September, distributing fertilizer once every 2-3 weeks.

Repotting: repotting the weeping willow will be carried out twice a year, in March and July, by cutting and ordering the roots.

Soil: as a soil it is better to use a mixture composed of clay, sand and peat in equal proportions.

Pruning: branches and shoots should be pruned between spring and summer, during the reporting period.: branches and shoots must be pruned between spring and summer, during the repotting period.

Binding: it is good to carry out the operation in March, on robust branches and shoots. The use of metal wire covered with paper is recommended.

Multiplication: the most suitable method for obtaining other willows is multiplication by seed.

PODOCARPO (PODOCARPUS MACROPHYLLA)

Family: podocarpaceae

Description: it is a subtropical tree, originating in Japan and China, it has a dark trunk and horizontal branches that carry thick tufts of needles.

Flowering: during the end of summer, rod-like fruits begin to develop.

Environment and exposure: it must be kept in a bright place, however far from direct sunlight. In summer it can be taken outside, left in a shady and ventilated place. During the winter it should be placed indoors at a temperature between 15 and 20 degrees Celsius - 59-68 F.

Watering: given its needle-like structure, it is sufficient to water mamatura: moderately throughout the year, to keep the soil always moist.

Fertilization: for the period between March and October it can be fertilized once every 2 weeks. In winter, however, it will be necessary to slow down the fertilization to once every 4-5 weeks.

Repotting: it is recommended every 2 years, when spring arrives, sprouting and shortening long roots.

Soil: the most suitable mixture for Podocarp is made up of sand, clay and peat in equal proportions.

Pruning: the branches can be pruned throughout the year, the shoots, however, must be sprouted to a length of 2 inch when they have reached 2-3 inch.

Binding: the application of the metal wire is always possible on completely lignified shoots branches.

Multiplication: methods of multiplication by seed or by cuttings are recommended.

POMEGRANATE (PUNICA GRANATUM NANA)

Family: punicaceae

Description: Pomegranate is a shrub native to the Mediterranean coastal areas. It is characterized by elongated, dark green deciduous leaves.

Flowering: in the period from August to September, small red-orange flowers and consequently reddish fruits begin to appear.

Environment and exposure: it can be kept all year inside, in a well-ventilated and well-lit place. In the summer, when it is not excessively hot, it must be kept in cool temperatures, between 5 and 10 degrees Celsius 41-50 F. If you keep it a little warmer, around 15 degrees Celsius - 59 F., the Pomegranate will tend to grow tall.

Watering: throughout the summer, especially if it is hot, it is good to water often and in abundance. At the arrival of winter, the frequency and doses should be reduced.

Fertilization: it is recommended only during the period from March to September, with liquid fertilizer for bonsai, administered once every 2 weeks.

Repotting: it is good spring, taking care to sprout and cut too long roots.

Soil: Pomegranate prefers a soil consisting of sand, clay and Pet in equal proportions.

Pruning: branches can be pruned throughout the year, while shoots will be sprouted in 1-2 pairs of leaves only when they have reached the number of 5-6 pairs. The buds from which you want the flowers to grow will not be clipped.

Binding: it is recommended to practice the application of the metal wire throughout the year, but not during the flowering period.

Multiplication: the most suitable methods for obtaining new seedlings are those by cutting and by seed. it can also be outside in the sun. In winter and in dwarfs. and repotting once every two years.

QUINCE (MALUS BACCATA)

Family: Rosaceae

Description: It is a tree native to Asia Minor, widespread throughout Europe. It is characterized by oval leaves and fruits similar to sour apples, but very fragrant.

Flowering: In spring, pinkish-white flowers come together in bunches.

Environment and exposure: It must always be kept in a very bright area but not exposed to direct sun. If it's inside, it is recommended to place it next to a window. Outside, from June to August, it can be positioned in dim light. For the winter we recommend a temperature between 10 and 15 degrees Celsius – 50-59 F..

Watering: Quince needs abundant and regular watering throughout the year, trying to keep the soil constantly humid.

Fertilization: In the period before flowering it can be fertilized once a week. Afterward, until October, it is good to let 2 weeks ago by before fertilizing again.

Repotting: Repotting can be practiced once every year, at the beginning of spring. It is good to cut and sprout overgrown roots.

Soil: We recommend a mixture consisting of sand, peat and clay in equal proportions.

Pruning: It is preferable to prune the branches in the period following flowering, while the shoots must be sprouted during the spring.

Binding: The application of the wire is recommended especially in summer on well-lignified branches and shoots.

Multiplication: The best methods to obtain new seedlings are above all the multiplication by seed and the development by cutting.

ROSEMARY (ROSAMRINUS OFFICINALIS)

Family: labiate

Description: it is an aromatic shrub, native to the Mediterranean regions. It has a dark brown wrinkled trunk and fragrant thin and elongated leaves.

Flowering: around mid-July produces blue flowers.

Environment and exposure: Rosemary should be placed near a bright window. In summer it can be placed outdoors, even in the sun. For the winter we recommend a temperature between 8 and 12 degrees Celsius - 46-53 F..

Watering: between spring and autumn it can be watered regularly, keeping the soil moist. In winter it is sufficient not to leave the soil dry for too long.

Fertilization: it is recommended to fertilize in the period between March and October, using fertilizer once every 2-3 weeks and stopping during flowering and in winter.

Repotting: repotting is necessary once every 2-3 years, towards the end of spring, slightly sprouting the roots.

Soil: it is advisable to use a mixture consisting of 2/5 of clay, 2/5 of peat and 1/5 of sand.

Pruning: pruning of the branches must be done in early spring, while the shoots can be topped throughout the year.

Binding: you can bind it all year round, as long as you make sure that the branches have the right strength.

Multiplication: the easiest method to obtain a new plant is by cutting.

RUBBER FIG (FICUS MICROCARPA)

Family: moraceae

Description: it is a large tree, coming from South East Asia. It has a robust trunk and branches, leathery leaves and a bright dark green.

Environment and exposure: throughout the year it can be kept in a bright and warm place, even if not in direct sunlight. In winter it prefers temperatures that are around 20 degrees Celsius - 68 F.

Watering: during the summer and in the vegetative period, it is better to water abundantly; more rarely in winter, in dry soil.

Fertilization: liquid fertilizer is recommended every 2 weeks in the period between March and September. In winter it is better to feed the fertilizer every month.

Repotting: repotting should be practiced once every year, during the beginning of spring, by cutting and shortening the too long roots

Soil: the ideal mixture is made up of 1/5 clay, 2/5 sand, 2/5 peat.

Pruning: the branches can always be cut, even in this case, as for the euphorbia, latex will come out. The buds will be shortened to 2-3 leaves.

Binding: can be practiced on branches and shoots, the latter, however, must already be robust enough.

Multiplication: cutting and air layering are recommended.

SAGEREZIA (SAGEREZIA THEEZANS)

Family: rhamnaceae

Description: Sagerezia is a tropical shrub, native to the southern part of China. It has a trunk with a dark-spotted color and leaves with a bright light green color.

Flowering: in summer, small tender flowers of white-yellow color begin to grow in the axils of the leaves.

Environment and exposure: it is possible to keep Segerezia at home all year round, near a bright window. In the summer it can be taken outdoors, leaving it even in the sun, if this is not too intense. In winter it prefers temperatures between 10 and 15 degrees Celsius - 50-59 F.

Watering: For the summer period it is advisable to water abundantly, sometimes by wetting the leaves. In winter it will be sufficient to keep the soil moist, however, if the temperature is hot, it will be necessary to spray.

Fertilization: fertilization must be carried out especially in the period between March and October, using liquid fertilizer once every 2 weeks. In winter, only if it is warm will fertilization be reduced to once every 4 weeks.

Repotting: it is recommended to practice repotting every year, or once every two years, always at the beginning of spring, cutting and shortening the roots.

Soil: the ideal proportions for obtaining a good soil for Sagerezia are made up of 2/5 of clay, 2/5 of peat and 1/5 of sand.

Pruning: the branches can be pruned throughout the year. The shoots, however, should be trimmed only if they have reached a number of leaves of 4-5 pairs, reducing them to 1-2 pairs. By cutting the buds, the development of the flowers is prevented.

Binding: to be practiced exclusively on lignified shoots and branches, but not during the flowering period.

Multiplication: the ideal method for better success is by cutting.

SCHEFFLERA (SCHEFFLERA ACTINOPHYLLA)

Family: araliaceae

Description: evergreen tropical tree from areas of Australia. It has a thin trunk with little branching and broad petiolate light green leaves. Easily produces aerial roots.

Environment and exposure: it is recommended to keep the plant in a bright and sunny place throughout the year. During the winter the temperature must be between 18 and 20 degrees Celsius - 64-68 F..

Watering: for the Schefflera it is sufficient to keep the soil at a constant humidity, without exceedingly too much when watering.

Fertilization: the fertilizer must be distributed throughout the year, once every 3-4 weeks.

Repotting: it is recommended to practice repotting once every 2-3 years, during the months of March-April, shortening overgrown roots.

Soil: the ideal mixture to be used consists of 1/5 of clay, 2/5 of peat and 2/5 of sand.

Pruning: branches and shoots can be pruned throughout the year.

Binding: given the particular structure of the Schefflera, binding is not recommended.

Multiplication: to obtain new seedlings it is advisable to follow the methods by seed, to be planted in spring, and by cutting, throughout the year.

TEA (CARMONA MICROPHYLLA)

Family: teaceae

Description: it is an evergreen tropical shrub, coming from southern Asia and China. It is characterized by a brown-gray trunk and oval bright green leaves.

Flowering: in the period between March and September, small white and fragrant flowers develop on the branches and, subsequently, reddish berries.

Environment and exposure: the tea plant can be kept indoors all year round, in a bright and ventilated place. In the summer it can be placed outdoors, without however exposing it to too direct sun. For the winter with temperatures between 15 and 20 degrees Celsius - 59-68 F..

Watering: in summer, or if the plant is placed in a warm place it is necessary to water abundantly and often, however, to prevent the soil from drying out. Sometimes the leaves can be sprayed.

Fertilization: for the entire period between spring and autumn it is possible to fertilize once every 2-3 weeks, however, it is necessary to interrupt the operation during flowering. In winter, fertilize only once every 6 weeks.

Repotting: repotting is recommended once every 2 years, during the spring, by cutting and potting

Soil: the ideal mixture for the tea plant is made up of 1/4 clay, 2/4 peat and 1/4 sand.

Pruning: the branches can be pruned at any time of the year, while the shoots must be shortened to 2-3 pairs of leaves when they have reached 5-6 pairs.

Binding: branches and shoots can be tied throughout the year as long as they are well lignified. However, tying is not always necessary, given the structure of the plant.

Multiplication: the recommended methods for the development of new plants are by seed and by cutting.

WEPPING WILLOW (SALIX REPENS)

Family: salicaceae

Description: this tree is indigenous to Asia and parts of Europe. The branches arch and hang loosely but gracefully. Young leaves have a silken texture on each side. Catkins adorn the tree in mid-spring

Flowering: flowers appear before the leaves emerge.

Environment and exposure: the weeping willow prefers warm temperatures and humidity, and should not be exposed to frost. The branches of the weeping willow can be brittle and delicate, therefore, they should not be placed in a windy area, should be placed in an outdoor area that receives abundant sunlight, but not too much direct sunlight in the hottest months. The leaves of the willow Bonsai can be susceptible to burning if let in too much direct sunlight. On hot days, or periods of extended heat, it is best to place the tree somewhere where it will be sunlight in either the morning or afternoon.

Watering: on hot summer days the willow needs huge amounts of water and must be watered several times a day. Never let the soil dry out. Water less in winter but keep the rootball slightly moist.

Fertilization: apply solid organic fertilizer every six weeks or use a liquid fertilizer every two weeks during the growing season. Don't feed with high nitrogen which would cause large leaves, long internodes and increased susceptibility to insects.

Repotting: Young plants may require re-potting twice in one year because of its rapid rate of growth. Older plants can be re-potted less often. Soil of good drainage and rich, organic matter will ensure successful growth.

Soil: the best soil for Weeping Willow bonsai trees, as well as most bonsai trees, is a sandy clay soil. This type of soil can hold water and nutrients and will also drain the excess away from the roots. Sandy clay soil also improves aeration and will help move oxygen to the roots to further boost tree health.

Pruning: this tree grow very quickly and require constant pruning to not "over grow". You will also need to cut growth back to the main branch every fall once the growing season is over.

Binding:Wiring every branch of your weeping willow will keep it in shape. The wood on a weeping willow is pretty soft, so you should wire the willow loosely to avoid scarring. To get the weeping effect, some branches may require a guy wire to train them down.

The branches are flexible and will bend well without snapping, but because the willow is such a fast grower, you may need to move and adjust the wires frequently

Multiplication: Willows are easily propagated from cuttings. They will even root in a glass of water. Even quite large and thick plant parts can produce roots.

WHITE-FIR (ABIES ALBA)

Family: pinaceae

Description: A resinous tree with a pyramidal crown native to the central and northern areas of Europe. It has an ash brown bark, cracked with horizontal branches. The leaves are flat with two whitish lines between the ribs of the lower face. It produces elongated and cylindrical pinecones.

Environment and exposure: It can be kept near a bright window, but not in the sun. In summer it is advisable to put it outside in the penumbra. The ideal temperature for the winter is between 10 and 15 degrees Celsius - 50-59F..

Watering: Throughout the summer the watering must be abundant, to reduce it in the winter period, always avoiding that the soil dries too much.

Fertilization: In the period from March to October it is recommended to fertilize once every 2 weeks, with liquid fertilizer; when winter comes the fertilizer will be used once every 4 weeks.

Repotting: Repotting must always be practiced once every 2 years, in the spring period before budding. It is necessary to cut and sprout the roots.

Soil: It is recommended to prepare a mixture containing 1/4 of clay, 2/4 of peat and 1/4 of sand.

Pruning: It is advisable to prune the branches in early spring, although they can be pruned throughout the year. The shoots should be shortened to 1 inch when they have reached a length of 1.5inches.

Binding: Tying can be practiced throughout the year. However, care must be taken that the affected branches and shoots are sufficiently robust.

Multiplication: The most suitable methods for obtaining new plants are the one by seed and the one by cutting

CONCLUSION

The art of keeping bonsais must be one of the most rewarding practices in the world today and even though it can take years of your life, it isn't something that you will ever regret doing. Growing bonsais is so much more than just growing a beautiful tree in a pot and looking after it on a daily basis; it is more of a choice that teaches you everything that you need to know about yourself.

It may be difficult to consider that growing a bonsai can take years and once you have shaped, nurtured, and helped grow it into something that you are truly proud of, it may have taken decades of your life. But when you look at the marvelous creations in front of you and your designing capabilities, you will know it was all worth it.

There will be times that you feel that you don't have the patience to perform this type of task but you will surprise yourself as you find yourself becoming more and more at peace with your newfound understanding.

There is a lot of detail in this book and even though you may feel overwhelmed at first, this book is merely just the beginning but it will help guide you along your way. Once you understand the basics of keeping bonsais at a beginner level, there will be nothing stopping you from exploring more difficult and advanced concepts.

Start with single styles and then move into group styles because you need to understand how to safely work with the roots of one tree before you move into dealing with multiple, and treat every individual bonsai that you have with all of the love and patience that you are building within yourself.

All of this will take practice and you are going to make mistakes, but that is the entire process of learning. Once you realize what you are capable of doing, you will want to do more and achieve more with growing these pieces of art.

This is a long journey that you are going to go on and even though it is one of growing trees in pots, it is more about self-discovery and it definitely is one that you are going to love to go on.

REFERENCES

Bonsai Empire. (n.d). *Air Layering: Cultivating Bonsai Trees from Air Layers.* Tree Cultivation. https://www.bonsaiempire.com/basics/cultivation/air-layering

Bonsai Empire. (n.d). *Bonsai Styles: Styles, Shapes, and Forms Explained.* Inspiration. https://www.bonsaiempire.com/origin/bonsai-styles

Bonsai Empire. (n.d). *Collecting Trees from the Forest.* Tree Cultivation. https://www.bonsaiempire.com/basics/cultivation/collecting-trees

Bonsai Empire. (n.d). *Grafting Trees.* Tree Cultivation. https://www.bonsaiempire.com/basics/cultivation/grafting-trees

Bonsai Empire. (n.d). *Growing a Bonsai from Cuttings.* Tree Cultivation. https://www.bonsaiempire.com/basics/cultivation/from-cuttings

Bonsai Empire. (n.d). *Growing Bonsai from Seed.* Tree Cultivation. https://www.bonsaiempire.com/basics/cultivation/from-seeds

Bonsai Empire. (n.d). *Repotting Bonsai: how to Repot Your Bonsai Tree.* Tree Cultivation. https://www.bonsaiempire.com/basics/bonsai-care/repotting

Bonsai Empire. (n.d). *Pruning Bonsai.* Techniques. https://www.bonsaiempire.com/basics/styling/pruning

Bonsai Empire. (n.d). *Shaping and Styling Bonsai Trees.* Techniques. https://www.bonsaiempire.com/basics/styling

Bonsai Empire. (n.d). *Wiring Bonsai Trees.* Techniques. https://www.bonsaiempire.com/basics/styling/wiring

REFERENCES FOR IMAGES

https://pixabay.com/photos/bonsai-tree-flowers-leaves-foliage-5872078/
https://www.pexels.com/photo/black-white-and-brown-caterpillar-on-green-grass-61148/
https://www.pexels.com/photo/bonsai-plant-1382195/
https://www.pexels.com/photo/crop-unrecognizable-woman-cutting-olives-on-tree-in-garden-6231905/
https://www.pexels.com/photo/green-and-brown-tree-beside-white-painted-wall-6738669/
https://www.pexels.com/photo/green-bonzai-tree-on-table-2149105/
https://www.pexels.com/photo/green-leafed-bonsai-plant-2977433/
https://www.pexels.com/photo/green-plant-on-brown-wooden-table-6876970/
https://www.pexels.com/photo/lady-cutting-tree-branch-with-secateurs-in-forest-6231832/
https://www.pexels.com/photo/person-in-red-jacket-and-brown-pants-holding-black-shovel-7656731/
https://www.pexels.com/photo/red-ants-on-green-leaf-3007693/
https://www.pexels.com/photo/shallow-focus-of-sprout-401213/
https://www.pexels.com/photo/snow-wood-winter-pot-7150414/
https://www.pexels.com/photo/white-flowers-in-blue-ceramic-pot-8280933/
https://www.pexels.com/photo/woman-putting-plants-on-pots-4751969/
https://www.pexels.com/photo/wood-garden-agriculture-farm-5919766/
https://www.pexels.com/photo/wood-light-sky-sunset-5982764/
https://pixabay.com/photos/adult-bonsai-hand-plant-portrait-1868109/
https://pixabay.com/photos/bonsai-larch-japan-culture-1805499/
https://pixabay.com/photos/bonsai-tree-winter-snow-ancient-3551706/
https://pixabay.com/photos/japan-tree-oriental-decoration-995393/
https://pixabay.com/photos/bonsai-tree-nature-plant-green-2149676/
https://pixabay.com/photos/transfer-tools-set-6082801/
https://pixabay.com/photos/bonsai-tree-japanese-green-2347165/
https://pixabay.com/photos/cord-yarn-floristry-tree-of-life-5400450/

Dear Reader

I am an emerging writer and, with the sales made by the book, I can continue my studies to publish other books on the subject.

I would appreciate an honest review from you by clicking here.

Also, please if you notice any mistakes or missing information, feel free to contact me at this e-mail address: daring.limited@gmail.com

Thank you for your support

Printed in Great Britain
by Amazon